PAT ON THE BACK

The Story of Pat Eddery

Also by Claude Duval
LESTER: A Biography

Pat on the Back
The Story of Pat Eddery

Claude Duval

Stanley Paul, London

Stanley Paul & Co Ltd
3 Fitzroy Square, London W1

An imprint of the Hutchinson Publishing Group

London Melbourne Sydney Auckland
Wellington Johannesburg and agencies
throughout the world

First published 1976
© Claude Duval 1976
Photographs © E. D. Byrne/Gerry Cranham/
Press Association/Sport & General/
Syndication International 1976

Set in Monotype Baskerville

Printed in Great Britain by The Anchor Press Ltd
and bound by Wm Brendon & Son Ltd
both of Tiptree, Essex

ISBN 0 09 126240 2

Contents

Acknowledgements

My sincere thanks are due to countless people in racing who have helped me write this biography of the champion jockey, Pat Eddery – not least the subject himself who gave me so much friendly assistance when recalling the many highlights of his short, but highly successful, career. His father, Jimmy Eddery, Frenchie Nicholson and Peter Walwyn – the men who have really fashioned his success – were also most helpful. It would be impossible to mention all the other people who have also helped but I must not fail to acknowledge with gratitude the assistance of trainers Michael Pope and Geoffrey Barling. So many other people, such as Keith Freeman, the man who bought Grundy, were extremely generous in giving me their time as I pieced together the contemporary racing jigsaw around the remarkable young Irishman. My press colleagues were especially kind. Richard Onslow's unique library, which is virtually a complete history of racing, was invaluable and so, too, were the many hours spent watching the video films of Jonathan Powell, reliving the magic moments of Pat's greatest triumphs. Colleagues Peter O'Sullevan, Brough Scott and Chris Poole were also extremely helpful. Photographers Gerry Cranham and Ed Byrne went out of their way to secure the best visual records of this young man, while thanks are finally also due to Beverley Frankland for re-typing the manuscript.

Introduction

'Bugger that' . . . was the emphatic reply from an unknown titch of an apprentice jockey in the weighing-room at Epsom in April 1969 when a valet handed him a brand new set of racing silks. 'Trample them on the floor,' advised one of the senior riders, 'it's bloody bad luck to wear new colours without getting them dirty.' But the apprentice, an innocent seventeen-year-old with choirboy looks to match, took no notice. He put on the bright, new shiny silks and went out to ride over the world-famous Derby course and distance. Ten minutes later he returned the still clean silks to the valet. He had ridden his first winner after fifty attempts. He had also defied one of racing's main superstitions and won on Alvaro.

His name was Patrick Eddery.

Just six years later the same modest youngster was back in the winners' enclosure at Epsom. But this time he had won the Derby on Grundy and was riding as the champion jockey. In this short time Eddery had rocketed to the very pinnacle of his profession. Statistically he gallops the turf of the world's racecourses on equal terms with that remarkable living legend, Lester Piggott.

To many, he is already better. Frankie Durr, that impish little muscleman, says: 'Lester is great, but so is Pat. I rate them as equal but Pat has time on his side. If he has no weight problems he should be champion for bloody years.' Trainer Duncan Sasse goes further and says: 'Eddery is the better of the two. He makes fewer mistakes.' Comparing Eddery to Piggott may be like trying to find another sun in the sky but it is worth noting the hurricane pace the young Irishman has set.

In the first seven years of his career Eddery rode 651 winners in England. In the same period Piggott rode 272. It took Lester seven years before he topped the magical century. Pat topped the 'ton' after only five seasons.

Peter Walwyn, the genius who has supplied so much of the ammunition for Eddery to blast his rivals, says: 'Lester has tremendous cunning and strength gained by years of experience. But don't forget that he was twenty-five when he first became champion. Pat was only twenty-two when he first did it.'

Having scaled the dizzy heights so quickly Pat admits: 'I often think how terrible it would be if I came sliding down the ladder.' With Frenchie Nicholson and Walwyn as his advisors there seems little chance of this. As he is still so young, a lengthy career stretches out before him and many records could be galloped past on the way.

Pat says: 'When I first rode Alvaro I didn't take any notice of the jockeys' theory that you should never wear clean silks. That seemed a load of rubbish to me. I go against another superstition in racing and often wear green clothes, although I have stuck to Frenchie Nicholson's advice and never bought a green car.

'I'm not like many jockeys who wear the same suits as they did when they won on some big race winner the time before. With Alvaro I wasn't going to bugger around jumping up and down on the colours. All I wanted to do was to ride winners.'

A simple ambition. One which he has been fulfilling ever since.

1. A Champion's Pedigree

Champion jockeys are not born. They are often bred through many generations to reach the very pinnacle of their gruelling profession. Lester Piggott is the Classic king – and the classic example. It is well known that his family have been training and riding winners for nearly 200 years. Relations on his mother's side have been starring in the sport for well over 100 years. The poker-faced maestro is directly descended from families like the Days, Cannons and Rickabys. In more recent times Lester's more immediate relations have always kept the family name bang in the racing limelight. Small wonder that the boy who was born on Guy Fawkes' Night at Wantage in 1935 was destined to follow in his family's illustrious footsteps.

'He's ruddy well bred to be a champion.' I can well recall the thunderous voice of Ryan Price in my ear at Lingfield one day when I was discussing with him his new stable jockey, Tony Murray. He is, of course, the son of the former National Hunt jockey Paddy Murray, who rode many winners for Reg Hobbs over hurdles and fences just after the war. So Murray, too, has racing blood in his veins.

Pat Eddery has the perfect blend. His father Jimmy Eddery was champion jockey of Ireland and his maternal grandfather, Jack Moylan, rode several Classic winners. Pat's family tree is not dotted with quite so many champion branches as Lester but all the right ingredients for success are clearly there. It is the way events over the years have fashioned Pat's success story which makes for so much interest. Racegoers watching this placid jockey strolling out to the parade ring on any afternoon throughout the summer months can scarcely guess how very different his life could have been.

It really started before the war in the hunting fields of lush, green-carpeted County Cork in the district near the small town of Doneraile. A youngster, barely twelve-and-a-half years old, caught the eye of a local landowner for the zest and skill he showed on an old pony. When the kid said he wanted to go into a racing stable the lady, Mrs Johnson, wrote to Irishman Atty Persse, who was at that time training at Stockbridge in Hampshire. Persse agreed to take the boy and only one week after he had left school he set out on the journey, which must have seemed like a trip to the other end of the earth, as he had barely been out of County Cork previously. It was the ability to shine on an old pony in the local hunt meetings which sparked off this trip.

Weighing only 4 st 3 lb and standing barely over four-and-a-half feet this little figure looked far from happy as he boarded the boat at Cork for the then nine hour trip to Fishguard on the Pembroke coast of Wales. He had never been on a boat before in his life and was saying farewell to his parents for the first time. On his coat lapel was a big label. It read: 'Jimmy Eddery – to Mr Persse, Stockbridge, England.'

Looking back at the crossing to England Pat's father, Jimmy Eddery, whose family were 'horse people', now chuckles merrily to himself as he relates the story. But he was frightened out of his youthful and innocent wits at the time.

'We set out on April 1st of all days – All Fools' Day,' he recalls. 'I thought I was the fool after just a few minutes at sea. I was sea sick virtually all the way over as it was a very rough crossing. I hardly had the courage to look at the huge waves. I thought every minute was going to be my last.

'I was met by a Mrs French in London off the train from Fishguard and put on another train to Stockbridge. When I got to the other end a chap was waiting and as I came through the ticket barrier he spotted the label and realized I was the youngster who had come over to become a jockey. I had to crouch in the back of an old van as he drove me to the stables. I didn't have a penny to my name.'

The wheel of fortune has spun its full course for Eddery Senior. He is a typically happy-go-lucky Irishman who, as he enters the later stages of his life, cannot be mistaken for anything else but an ex-jockey. Having once been champion of Ireland, in 1975 he was working as an ordinary stable lad for Gordon Smyth at Lewes, riding out work every morning and doing all the chores the stable lads have to do.

Sipping a pint of his beloved Guinness in one of the Lewes hotels Jimmy, typically dressed in tweed jacket and riding breeches, said: 'Ironically my second ever ride for old Persse was on a horse called Tiddley Bits at Lewes. I was beaten a short head by the now Sir Gordon Richards.

'I cried like hell when I first arrived at Stockbridge. Atty Persse was hard as nails. He was an Irishman but he was also a slave driver when it came to the young lads. I was there for seven years and only had a fortnight's holiday. We slept in a dormitory which had iron bars outside the windows to keep us in. We were locked in the room every night. Some of the lads were allowed out one evening to go to a fairground. Half the buggers ran away. I was paid two bob a week and in the summer was up at 5.15 every morning. We worked through lunchtime, had a rest and then finished work at seven o'clock. They were hard times but somehow I don't regret them one little bit. Some of the other lads were always going down with 'flu but I managed to stay fit and well all the time I was there.

'My first ever ride on a racecourse was a little odd – I got no further than the paddock! We had a horse called Royal Flush who was a bit dodgy. He was bloody lively in fact. Because of this the guv'nor told me to ride him round in the parade ring before the race. This I did and then Steve Donoghue rode him in the actual race. My first winner came when I rode a horse called Aphrodite the Fourth to victory at the old Derby City course in a boys' race. They have closed the course since. I remember thinking to myself: "You'll get a few bob out of this." But I got sweet F.A. My next winner was for Lord Sefton again. They were hard times and we got precious little money. I rode nine winners in England but was yearning to get back to Ireland. In 1943, when I was twenty, there was little racing in England because of the war so I took a chance. I don't want to say too much about it but let's just say that I got back to Ireland as quick as I could. A moonlight flit I suppose.

'I joined Darby Rogers who trained at the Curragh. I remember going down to Mallow one day and riding two horses for a chap I had never met or heard of beforehand. They both won over hurdles carrying 12 st 7 lb in tiny races worth about £100. The trainer was a young man from Churchtown, just seven miles from my home town. He didn't have more than a dozen horses and was just starting out. It was Vincent O'Brien, who was later to become one of the greatest trainers Ireland and indeed the world has ever known.

'In 1944 I had my first ever Classic ride and he proved to be a winner . . . or half a winner! I dead-heated in the Irish 2,000 Guineas at the Curragh on a horse called Good Morning. Jack Moylan rode the other one, who was called Slide On.

'Of course, in those days there was no such thing as a photo finish. I thought that I was beaten and to this day I am positive that Jack beat me in that race. I was highly surprised when the judge announced that it was a dead-heat.

'I used to see old Jack and his family when I went to Mass. I met his daughter Josephine and we were subsequently married. It was the joining of two racing families and I was very fortunate. Around this time I was based at Osborne Lodge on the Curragh and riding for a trainer called Ginger Wellesley. Actually he was supposed to be called the Honourable Wellesley but no bugger ever called him that. He was always known as Ginger because of his bright red hair. He was supposed to be a direct descendant of the Duke of Wellington! These were good times for me and I was riding plenty of winners.'

How many times was he actually champion of Ireland? 'Put down once, that will be enough,' said Jimmy with a grin. 'Christ, I was second in the championship about a million times. I was the permanent runner-up, or that's what it felt like.'

It was when Jimmy joined the all-conquering stable of wealthy Seamus McGrath at Glencairn, Cabinteely, County Dublin that he really hit the high spots. As jockey, and then assistant trainer, Jimmy was associated with the McGraths for twenty-four years and this partnership paved the way for his son Pat Eddery to become apprenticed there a few years later.

Says Jimmy, whose ruddy face betrays many an icy dawn-light gallop: 'I had my first ever ride in the Epsom Derby in 1955. I rode Panaslipper for Mr McGrath while Lester Piggott rode our other horse called Windsor Sun. He was about 33–1 but I was the 100–1 outsider. Actually I never had the choice of rides, I was told which of the two I would partner. Anyway I would have gone for Panaslipper. He was the better of the two but had a setback in his training just prior to the Derby and was not quite right. He just tired and faded in the final stages and eventually we finished second to Phil Drake. I was only beaten 1½ lengths and was not too disappointed considering that it was my first ever ride in the Derby. My first outright Classic winner was when I rode Stalino to win the Irish 2,000 Guineas in 1945. Possibly I was lucky to be second on Panaslipper as I am sure the ante-post favourite, Hugh Lupus, would have won for Rae Johnstone but he was taken out because of an injury.

'Still Panaslipper did go on to win the Irish Derby in his next race and I can tell you that he was one hell of a horse. On his day he was a world-beater and my proud boast is that I was never beaten on him in Ireland. We were unbeatable. He wasn't the best horse I ever rode, however, that would have to be Arctic Chevalier. He only ran twice but was absolutely brilliant. Sadly he broke down after splitting a pastern and never raced again.

'In 1957 I really fancied my chances of winning the English 1,000 Guineas and Epsom Oaks on Silken Glider, the best filly I ever rode. But at Newmarket she hung very badly and we finished fifth behind Harry Carr on Lady Zia Wernher's Meld, who was strongly fancied and backed down to 11–4.

'Silken Glider was a top-class filly but was very difficult to ride. Without wishing to be unkind, she was in fact a bit of a bitch. Still I fancied her to land the Oaks. People always say that the greatest race Lester Piggott ever rode was on the Queen's Carrozza in the Oaks that day and I can vouch for that. Christ, you never saw a man get so much out of a horse as that day. He was really inspired and it was just my luck to meet him in that mood. He was 100–8 while I was 20–1 on Silken Glider.

'We had a right old battle in the closing stages and as we went past I was certain I had won. It was one of the very first times that a camera was in operation for the finish and I was happy and pretty certain I had got the nod. Lester Piggott thought he had lost and so did Noel Murless, Carrozza's trainer. But Seamus McGrath thought that we had just lost and he was right – I had lost by a short head. To this day I still think it was very debatable, although I have never actually seen the photograph. It would bring back unhappy memories. I only lost really because Silken Glider was such a difficult mare to ride and in the final stages, just like Newmarket, she hung up the hill. Lester was always on the inside. I was lucky in a way as Frankie Durr was on the favourite, Even Star, and I just beat him for a run and he never really got to us. Still as with Panaslipper I went back to Ireland and had better luck as Silken Glider did win a non-sponsored Irish Oaks.

'One of the happiest moments of my life was watching Patrick winning the Oaks in 1974 on Polygamy. I went down to my local for a few brandies that night, I can tell you. Good job I didn't have to ride out next morning!

'The McGraths were great employers. If you are with one family for twenty-four years they have got to be good. I retired as a jockey in June, 1959 after a controversial race at Gowran. I was riding an outsider called Ballymaster, who was any price you like. It was on the round track and there was a bit of bumping and boring. Also in the race were Liam Ward, Garnet Bougoure and several other top Irish-based jockeys. I was pipped by a short head but was immediately summoned into the Stewards' room. I was accused of bumping in to the others on purpose. But it was ridiculous, the other chaps who complained had no chance of winning the race. Still I got into trouble and the very next day Mr McGrath came up to me and said: "I think you should retire."

'I agreed to but continued working as his assistant and as an all-rounder until 1966 when I took over the Railway Hotel in Kildare. It was a mistake and I would never venture into trade again. I'll stay this side of the bar quite happily but I'll never again step the other side.'

Jimmy has been back to his native country many times since he joined Gordon Smyth's stable. But he admits in his Irish accent: 'I did watch the Irish Derby in 1973 when I thought Pitcairn should have trotted up. But I kept myself to myself and kept out of the way. I was also there when Patrick won the Irish Derby on Grundy.'

Puffing away merrily at a cigarette Jimmy recalls with pride his career as a top Irish rider. He always refers to his son as Patrick – 'I never call him Pat.' He still owns a house bang next-door to his old hotel in Kildare, the town made famous for the exploits of Paddy Prendergast and other top Irish trainers. 'I may well go back there one day,' he reflects but does not seem wildly excited about the prospect.

'When I packed up the hotel I knew that I would have to get back into racing. It was in my blood,' he said. 'I did have a word with Joe Mercer and was at one time trying to get fixed up with Dick Hern but he did not have a vacancy at the right time. Instead I saw an advertisement in the *Sporting Life* from Mr Smyth. I came over and got the job. It's funny really that I should work at Lewes after having one of my early rides on the former racecourse. I didn't have a penny when I first came to England and the wheel has now gone right round. But I am happy with life generally. I love horses and being in the racing game.'

Unnoticed by racing crowds unless they actually know him, Jimmy often lead horses trained by Gordon Smyth round the parade rings and paddocks. On occasions his son Patrick walked by to join his respective owners and trainers. One was at the top of his profession. The other had already made his contribution. Their jobs are now both with horses – but worlds apart.

When Gordon Smyth reduced his string for 1976 Jimmy had to find a new job and was expecting a move to Malton in Yorkshire.

Says Jimmy: 'I never rave too highly about Patrick's riding. I still think that Lester Piggott is the best jockey I have ever seen. He is unique. But I would place Patrick second on my list and as he is still young, he can only get better.'

And with one of his inquiring glances he adds: 'I hope that doesn't sound too biased.' Not at all. It is the opinion not only of a rightly proud father but of an increasing number of people.

2. 'I knew what I wanted . . .'

History often repeats itself in real life and it is often the case in racing. Jimmy Eddery was a champion jockey before his son Patrick followed in his footsteps. Father Jimmy was one of twelve children – six boys and six girls. Coincidentally Pat is also one of twelve children – six boys and six girls. But strictly speaking Pat is one of thirteen children born to Mrs Josephine Eddery. For his parents' first ever child died after nineteen months of Pink's disease. Relates Jimmy sadly: 'He would have been the eldest in the family and we christened him James after me. Who knows, he could have been riding alongside Patrick in the big races these days.'

John is now the eldest of the Eddery brood. He was once with Arthur Stephenson, the highly talented Bishop Auckland trainer who regularly saddles a century of jump winners each season with the ease of Geoff Boycott scoring a 'ton' against a second-rate bowling attack. John was keen to follow in the Eddery racing footsteps but became too heavy and is now a barman in a Dublin public house. Second son of the Eddery family is Michael, who set out as a jump jockey in the north and was doing extremely well until he had the tragic accident at Newcastle in November 1972 when, after a crashing fall, he had to have his right leg amputated below the knee.

Patrick is the third eldest son and the fifth of the Eddery children. His younger brother Robert – he is eight years younger – has just started out as an apprentice with Kevin Prendergast at the Curragh.

Youngest of the Eddery boys are Paul and David, who live at home with their likable parents. Comments Jimmy:

'Racing on the whole has been good to me and I would not stand in their way if they wanted to follow the others and try to become jockeys.'

Mary, Olive, Magdalen, Deidre, Stella and Josephine are Pat's sisters. It is Olive, a cheerful brunette, who is closest to him. She and her husband Terry live with Pat at his Cheltenham home and it is Terry who acts as his chauffeur for the lengthy journeys he has to make to attend various race meetings. Terry was much needed when young Pat was 'warned off' for four endorsements for speeding but now does the job regularly. He jokes: 'Pat just gets straight into the car and goes straight to sleep. I have never known anybody who can relax so easily. Riding over 700 races a year is extremely tiring but Pat is lucky in that he can switch off in a second and relax.'

Born into a household dominated by the famous father's job in racing it was heavily odds-on that young Pat would take an interest in the sport. Like his arch rival Lester Piggott he showed little interest in school. His first love was horses and he could not wait for the day when he was apprenticed into a full racing stable.

Recalls Jimmy: 'Patrick was learning to ride virtually before he could learn to walk. We had this old pony and I used to stick him up on him. He was a hard old bastard and would eat a table if he got half a chance. He used to eat anything. Not surprisingly he was well muscled and one dared not put up any young mug on him. But even at an early age Patrick got on well with him.

'Patrick was born in Dublin but we lived just outside the town in the little town of Blackrock. He was born on March 18th, 1952. Lester Piggott had ridden his first winner at Haydock in August, 1948 . . . four years before Patrick was even born. An old pal of Joe McGrath, Seamus's father, was a man called Paddy Drury, who used to do a lot of betting for him. He was a very good friend of mine so when Patrick came along I decided to call the boy after him. For years afterwards Paddy would send him a fiver on his birthday. He was fully christened Patrick James John.

'By the time he was four years old Patrick was crazy about

horses and actually had his own pony. Soon he was asking me when he could ride a racehorse at Mr McGrath's place as he often used to come along to watch me riding work, particularly on Saturdays, when he had a day off from school. By the time he was nine he was allowed to ride racehorses at exercise.'

Admits Pat: 'At school I did not give a damn for lessons, especially after I knew how to read and write. That was enough for me. I knew what I wanted to do and I wanted to get on and do it. I must confess that I never did much studying. Cycling the three miles out to Mr McGrath's stables was the big love of my life.

'At that age I had one recurring dream. It seems crazy now looking back but I was forever dreaming that one day I would be a champion jockey and that I would win the Derby. I dreamt that over and over again. It used to be quite disappointing to wake up and find that it was all a dream. I suppose the best horse I ever rode out when I was at the McGraths' was Ballyciptic.'

By the time he was fourteen Pat was able to leave school and become apprenticed to McGrath, which had been his sole aim ever since he watched his father riding work and saw him actually in action on the racecourse.

Says Jimmy: 'From the very first day he started Patrick was a great little worker. He had been riding out regularly but now he was on the staff and doing all the jobs stable lads have to do when they start in the game. He was always a happy-go-lucky child. A bit of a joker – that's how I remember him more than anything else. He was a right little wise-cracker, always having the comical things to say at the right time. Also working in the yard at that time was Oliver Gray. Patrick was always the joker while Ollie was the serious one.'

Gray, again like Eddery, was given few chances to star in the saddle. 'There is not so much racing in Ireland as there is in England,' he says. 'I suppose I had ten rides for Mr McGrath in the three years I was there. I remember I had one second during that time. My first ride was on Rulartic, who finished in the middle of a decent field at Phoenix Park.

I was only sixteen years old when I had my first ride and weighed only 4 st 13 lb. I used to look after Levmoss the subsequent Arc winner.'

Realizing opportunities were few and far between in Ireland, Gray – also like his schoolboy buddy Eddery – mentioned to McGrath that he was not entirely happy. 'He was very good and gave the boys a ride in rotation when a suitable horse and race came along,' says Ollie, 'but the chances were not very often.'

Eddery had left for England a little before Gray, who finally opened his winning account when Go Too won by a short head at Edinburgh. Ollie was then twenty years old and had waited a long time to finally get into the winners' enclosure – but even then he did not officially make it. He recalls: 'I won by a short head but was certain at the time that I had been beaten. Just like when I was with Doug Smith and not very happy, especially with Levmoss winning the Arc, I couldn't believe my bad luck. Anyway I was certain that Go Too was beaten and rode into the runner's up position.'

Apprenticed in Ireland, whisked away to England as an unknown boy rider, and twenty years old before he finally rode a winner in Scotland. That's the Gray story but he has gone from strength to strength. He says; 'Pat became a champion and I am thrilled for him. I could always tell that he would get to the top, although he was always very modest. He was built to be a perfect rider even as a teenager. I was always on the small side and my mother used to stuff me full of potatoes and bread in an effort to make me put on weight. It all worked too well as I now have a job to do eight stone. I go up to over nine stone in the winter and my big problem in the future will be my weight. Virtually every day during the summer I have to put on a sweat suit and run round Middleham. Then whenever I can I have a sauna at the races or pop into Darlington. It's a far cry from the days when my mother used to pile my plate high. I have a similar problem to Lester Piggott but I hope to God I never look as drawn as he does on occasions when he has obviously been wasting.'

At least Gray did have to overcome one horror fall as a child. Jimmy recalls the occasion vividly: 'In 1956 I had been riding quite a few winners and was doing very nicely. Few people in Ireland at that time had decent cars but one day driving through Kildare I saw a posh German car for sale. I'm afraid I could not resist it. I dashed in and gave the chap cash for it. I think it was the first German car ever seen in Kildare at the time. One day I was driving from Kildare back to Dublin and picked up a friend and gave him a lift. When he got out he insisted on going into a shop and buying some chocolates for Patrick, who was only four at the time and was sitting in the back. When the other chap went I lifted Patrick into the front and off we went. I suppose I was doing about 60 mph when suddenly the door on his side flew open and he went flying out. I looked in the mirror and saw him flying up into the air. He came down with a terrible thump and was cut to bits. Remarkably he was not too badly hurt although very shaken. It appeared that this bloody car had doors which opened oddly and my friend had not closed the door correctly. God, was I glad when I picked him up off the road and realized that he was not as badly hurt as he could easily have been. It was a miracle he didn't break every bone in his body.

'Not many people fall out of a car at 60 mph and get away with only cuts and bruises. Even to this day when anybody ever talks to me about Patrick, I think to myself: 'Little do they know that but for that bit of luck on the road from Kildare to Dublin he could easily have never ridden a winner in his life.'

3. The Frenchie Nicholson Academy

Irish racing provided few opportunities for a young apprentice like Pat Eddery. His master, Seamus McGrath, realized that he had more than the average talent but there were not the openings. Seamus recalls: 'Pat quickly showed me that he had what it took to become a jockey. But there were few suitable horses and suitable races for a boy to ride in. Like others before him and after him he had to look elsewhere to really get on. I was sorry to see him go but delighted that he has achieved the success which has now come to him.'

Jimmy Eddery, who at the time Pat left Ireland was McGrath's assistant, can recall vividly Pat's first-ever ride on a racecourse but is certain that he should have ridden another horse prior to this, which turned out to be a winner. Says Jimmy: 'Pat used to mind a fair eight-year-old handicapper called Vale of Cliona. I thought that he was bound to ride him in a race just to get him started. But the guv'nor put up some other bloody buffer and he won as he liked. Patrick wasn't disappointed but I can remember being bloody mad at the time.'

Eventually the chance did come along for Eddery Jnr, but there was to be no fairy-tale start. On August 19th, 1967 Pat Eddery had his first and only ride in Ireland as an apprentice when he rode True Time in the Kildare Handicap over six furlongs at the Curragh. True Time was the 20–1 outsider of six runners. Recalls Pat: 'I was very nervous and they seemed to go one hell of a gallop. I was never really in the race.' At halfway it was clear that Eddery had no chance of making a winning debut. He finally finished last, tailed-off a long way behind the others. The race was won by Charlie

McGarritty on Gay Cloud, who had three quarters of a length to spare over Liam Ward, who was second on Michaelis with the 15–8 favourite Nameless Bug (Johnny Roe) third. Only five days before Eddery's disappointing first ride True Time had in fact trotted up in the Makel Maiden Plate at Gowran Park. This time he had been ridden by George McGrath, no relation of Seamus.

Oliver Gray says: 'Pat was all excited when he had the ride on True Time but was not too worried when he finished last.' Father Eddery believes his son was disappointed but was too mature to show his feelings. 'He was always a lad for keeping his feelings to himself,' says Jimmy, 'and that was certainly the case that day at the Curragh. God, I was chuffed when all those years later he went back to the Curragh and won the Irish 2,000 Guineas and Irish Derby on Grundy.'

It was soon clear to father and son Eddery that a move to England had to be made. Says Jimmy: 'It was Patrick who wanted to come. I had rather mixed feelings about it all but the youngster was especially keen to try his luck in England. Here again things could have turned out differently.

'Seamus McGrath was mad keen for Patrick to go over to Sir Gordon Richards' yard. I don't really know why but the move didn't take place. Either Gordon had his full quota of boys or was at the stage of his career when he was packing up training. I was glad anyway as I always pictured in my mind one man who would make all the difference for Patrick. I saw old Frenchie Nicholson ride and knew that he had a good reputation for steering apprentices in the right direction. We made the approach to Frenchie and he agreed to take Pat. His mother was not very happy about him leaving home and nearly broke down when he finally went.'

In 1935 when Jimmy Eddery came to England it was a hectic boat trip from Cork to Fishguard. When Pat Eddery travelled over it was in the comfort of a plane, accompanied by his father and just one case containing all his belongings. Recalls Pat: 'I must admit I hated it at first. I had never ever been away from home and I was rather nervous. But Mr Nicholson soon made me at home and I loved working with the horses.' The linking of Nicholson and Eddery in 1967 was without doubt the biggest single factor in the grooming of the now internationally famous jockey. Nicholson had already discovered one boy wonder in Paul Cook but Pat Eddery was to become his first champion jockey.

The Frenchie Nicholson apprentice academy can boast results second to none. To understand Eddery's success is to realize the wonderful training he received from Frenchie, ever his adviser, tutor and friend.

An unknown apprentice, who had finished tailed-off in his only race, and an ex-jockey, who never even rode on the Flat in England, hardly seem the right combination for glory on the Flat. And what makes the story even more remarkable is that Cheltenham, the very shrine of steeplechasing, was the place where it all started.

But Frenchie's life started near Rotherham, Yorkshire when he was born on January 13th, 1913. He told me: 'My father was a huntsman and when I was only twelve I went to work for some stables in France. I had never been out of England before. I was in France from 1925 for three years. I never rode around Chantilly but had a few rides at the country meetings. It did not take me very long to pick up the language. After that I came back to Epsom and had six years with Stanley Wootton.'

Jockeys who have had any contact with Frenchie will tell you affectionately that he's very hard and very fair. This was exactly Frenchie's description of the Stanley Wootton apprentice school which produced such famous names as Staff Ingham, Charlie Smirke and Jackie Sirett.

Says Frenchie: 'This was the best apprentice school in the world. Wootton was a brilliant trainer of horses – and boys. We only earned five bob a week but we had the best of everything. We learnt the lot. "Hard but fair" was his motto and he kept to it.'

Nicholson, a typically dour Yorkshireman who can give the impression of being fierce until a friendly smile beams across his face, never rode in a single race on the Flat in England in his life. He soon became too heavy for the Flat and had to switch to the jumps. The fact that he never rode on the Flat in England makes his success with apprentices all the more amazing.

Frenchie, who rode his first ever winner at Plumpton, became one of the best jump jockeys of all time. He won the 1942 Cheltenham Gold Cup on Medoc II and the 1936 Champion Hurdle on Victor Norman. A win on Tant Pis in the Imperial Cup in 1947 was among his many successes. Twice at Cheltenham he rode four winners in a day. John Sharratt, much respected senior racereader of *Raceform*, happily recalls the win of Medoc II. He told me: 'I was on leave from the RAF at the time and George Roberts, the jockeys' valet, persuaded me to give him a hand on the jockeys' trial scales. I overheard Roger Burford and Gerry Wilson discussing the Gold Cup. Gerry said "I think I know the winner. I saw old Frenchie Nicholson win a chase on Medoc II at Manchester the previous autumn when the going was so heavy it was up to their necks. As it is teeming down now that's the one I think will do it." After hearing this I dashed round and had a £1 on Frenchie and he duly produced the goods. A great jockey. And the money came in handy for an airman on leave at the time, I can tell you.' Sharratt, who has the rare ability to spot potential winners even in a twenty-eight runner maiden race at Newmarket, does not gamble now. Just before the 1975 Cheltenham Gold Cup I was amused to hear one pressman inquire from John which of the runners he had backed. Looking up from his work he quickly replied: 'I didn't back Arkle so how can I back any of these buggers?'

When Frenchie retired as a jockey he set himself up as a trainer just a furlong or two from his beloved Cheltenham racecourse. Park Corner, Prestbury was to be the spot where so many useful riders were to learn their far from easy art. Says Frenchie: 'I must admit that at one stage I was going downhill fast. I thought to myself "I must get some kids." It was when Dorothy Padget died that I really started to feel the pinch. She had thirty-five horses with me and when they left it meant that I lost a lot of work. I could hardly make a living training horses but I guessed that I could earn a few bob from having apprentices.

'People always ask me what my secret is. I tell them that I have been lucky. Let's face it, these kids have had some riding ability in them. I have just brought it out. It's no bloody good if the basic flair is not there. When a kid first comes to me I want him to have small feet, small hands, sharpness and a good outlook. But if he is not clean and tidy or has bad manners he has no chance whatsoever. He may as well go straight back home. Ideally I don't like them to have any experience. I made an exception with Pat Eddery and clearly he had learnt no bad habits so it was all okay. I realized pretty soon that Pat was going to make a jockey. From the word go he was a good trier.'

Having decided to depend on apprentices as much as training to make a living Frenchie was fortunate in that a young Cheltenham schoolboy was just about to leave school and was intent on becoming a jockey, principally because he was so small and no other profession looked open to him. It was a very nervous Paul Cook who penned a letter to Nicholson asking whether he could join his yard.

Recalls Paul Cook: 'I'll never forget the first time my father and I visited the guv'nor's yard to discuss me joining him. When we arrived he was mowing the lawn. We just stood there for what seemed like hours while he mowed the whole lawn. I was scared stiff when he finally walked over to us. But it all worked well and I signed on as an apprentice. I was paid £3 a week but Mr Nicholson was marvellous to me and even bought a horse called Balle-dor which was an ideal ride for an apprentice. I rode my first race at Bath and had plenty of seconds and thirds but no ruddy winners. I had over sixty rides before I finally had my first winner . . . and even then I did not finish first. It was in September, 1963 at Warwick when I rode a horse called March Fast. We finished second but the stewards held an inquiry and Joe Mercer had the race taken away from him and it was given to me.

'It's hard to explain just why Frenchie Nicholson has such great success with apprentices where so many other trainers fail. Basically he's hard. He's a bloody grafter and is quick to tell you that it's a hard game. He teaches you all the little things while Mrs Diane Nicholson is the formbook expert.

Although it was a hard life with the Nicholsons I loved every minute of it. We had plenty of laughs as well. When we were not working with the horses or in the yard the guv'nor soon found a job of fencing or hedge-cutting for us to do. A hard but fair grafter – that's Frenchie Nicholson.

'As I lived in Cheltenham I used to cycle to the yard every morning. It was a twelve mile a day round trip. I don't suppose many youngsters these days would be prepared to do this.'

Cook became a wonder boy. When he was still only a kid he was being hailed as a second Steve Donoghue. At the time he told reporters: 'I love speed. When I was at school I always tried to ride my bike faster than the other boys. This was probably because I was smaller than all the rest. I used to be thrown by horses on the gallops regular as clockwork when I started. Lester Piggott is my idol.'

When only nineteen Cook left Nicholson and became top jockey to Jack Jarvis at Newmarket in 1966. The world seemed to be at his feet. He looked well odds-on to succeed Lester Piggott as the champion jockey. He won his first Classic when the Irish-trained Glad Rags won the 1966 1,000 Guineas after steadily wearing down Berkeley Springs and beating her impressively. This made up for Cook's disappointment when Pretendre was beaten twenty-four hours earlier in the 2,000 Guineas. There was to be a further setback for the boy wonder when he was just pipped by veteran Scobie Breasley – more than twice his age – in the Derby on Charlottown. Here again Cook rode Pretendre and the winning margin was only a neck. These were the days when Cook's name was never far from the headlines. But disaster struck and he lost the Lord Rosebery retainer and his career started to nosedive. Admits Paul: 'Having been with Mr Nicholson and always under his eye I did miss his advice when I was left on my own.'

Cook was Nicholson's first success. Frenchie admits: 'If a lad does well he can come out of his time with about £6000.' This means that the apprentice master gets virtually the same amount as their rewards are usually shared. Cook was a good money-spinner.

Besides Paul Cook and Pat Eddery, Frenchie had a lot of time for Fred Messer in the early days. 'He was a very good rider but he became too heavy,' says Frenchie. Michael Dickinson, the beanpole-like son of the northern trainer Tony Dickinson, is another ex-Nicholson pupil. He is the tallest jockey riding today and still shows signs of fine horsemanship learnt from the Prestbury handler. The many millions of television racewatchers also see another former Nicholson trainee when they switch on. For Brough Scott, the ITV racing personality and *Sunday Times* racing correspondent, also started his racing days at Cheltenham.

Brough told me: 'Frenchie was a hard guv'nor but he has always had a childlike enthusiasm for the job. He could get annoyed but he wanted to share your success with you. He was very happy for you to do well. His maxim was always to do the little things well. "Have style and cut a dash" he would say. "Don't canter down to the start like any old bag." He was always telling me to be smart and neat and to keep my back straight. Another of his rules was always to go down to the start under the rail. Other jockeys may look as though they are tied on with string but you can always spot Frenchie's lads. They have come off a kind of production line which makes them the brigade of guards in racing. He knows what the apprentices should do and he does it right.

'Racing's a funny game. Everybody will be very nice to you when you are a jockey but the one thing they will never do is coach you – except Frenchie. They will probably just say "Watch another jockey" but Frenchie is forever saying: "That leg is too far round."

It was on the gallops that Frenchie was really at his best. When I first went there I thought that the path to Cleeve Hill was like some scramble up a mountain. He watches every gallop and is always on about "Sit up, hands down." If he thought you had the ability to be a jockey he would be on at you even more. He'd never stop sometimes.

'But Flat race jockeys can earn a lot of money in a short time and several have gone wrong when they have got out of this type of discipline. When I first went to Frenchie's to ride out Paul Cook was just beginning to set the racing world alight. I can remember him winning the Chester Cup but at six o'clock the next morning he was up and back at the yard mucking out. He was sometimes so tired he used to sleep on his way to the races. It was great riding out there. Frenchie's earthy enthusiasm was marvellous. At 6.45 you could hear him in a box mucking out and he'd come out and tell you "That's the third one I have done!" Like all sports he stressed that only hard work would pay results.'

Scott started out for Nicholson when he was seventeen – 'it must have been about then because I couldn't drive and had to get a lift to the yard.' He says: 'I lived near Broadway and Frenchie was the nearest trainer. Even in those days people used to say how good he was to apprentices. Tim Holland-Martin, who later bred Grundy for Pat Eddery to win the Derby, was the king of the local hunt. He used to ride out for Frenchie and that is why I first rang him up. I must admit that I was scared stiff of him at first. He was gruff in his manner but I think he secretly liked to put over the impression of being a hard man. I had just left public school and was going to Oxford University. It was made very clear to me that I was going to have to graft and not stand around like a wallflower. My first ever point-to-point ride turned out to be a winner when I won on Red Squirrel at Crowell, near Oxford. By then I was hooked on racing. I used to see Paul Cook at the stables. He was tiny, a mouse of a boy. Frenchie used to watch him bringing up the milk in the morning and say: "I'll make a jockey of him one day." He used to relate wonderful stories about Stanley Wootton and always finished up by saying "He had eyes like a hawk. Hard man." '

Scott admits 'After riding four point-to-point winners I wanted to ride against some of the professional legends. In the point-to-points they were mostly fat old amateurs. I had my first ride under rules on Tamlin at Woore Hunt. I sat at breakfast and Nicholson asked me "Have you schooled her?" as he was always very keen that none of his boys should ride a horse in a race which they had not sat on before. I was thrilled actually looking in the paper and seeing my name. I was crazy keen to do well, dangerously so. I drove an old mini van to the races – bloody miles away. It was the second division of some moderate novice hurdle. When I arrived at the weighing-room such names as Bobby Beasley, Johnny Gilbert, Tim Brookshaw and Terry Biddlecombe were all there. As we went towards the first hurdle we went downhill. My mare was a thoroughbred and I thought we were going a million miles an hour. I had never known anything go so fast. But when we jumped the first hurdle I was about 100 yards behind the leaders. Still we managed to finish and actually beat one on the run-in.

'My first ride for Frenchie was at Cheltenham on a horse called Articeelagh which my father had bought for about £700. He was an old shit really, a funny old bugger. You had to keep persevering on him. There were twenty-eight runners in this hurdle and Frenchie was marvellous before the race. He never left anything to the last minute in the paddock. He would always say the previous day "You know what to do, don't you?" He was a great one for saying "Look after yourself and keep kicking. Squeeze him along." At the top of the hill at Cheltenham my fella was not very interested but I saw Fred Winter in front of me dart up the inner. Then we started to go like a rocket and miracle of all miracles we finished third. I remember looking at Winter in the weighing-room. He was all muscle and looked more like a wrestler than a jockey. He'd won the race on the Ryan Price-trained Sky Pink.

'Articeelagh also gave me my first winner on the Flat. I rode him at Epsom and a bit of mud caught in his eye. Frenchie said: "I reckon the mud hit you in the eye." But we put blinkers on him at Lingfield and he pulled even in the parade ring. I had to choke him up like a motor bike all the way up the straight but we beat a 6–4 on hot-pot of Dick Hern's by a neck in a photo finish. It was after this win at Lingfield that my admiration and friendship with Frenchie was really cemented. He was always very much against his lads using the whip excessively. "Grab hold of them and crack 'em down the shoulder," was another of his golden rules. I can remember Paul Cook riding at Bath one day. He got to work with the whip and Frenchie did not like it at all. He refused to allow him to carry a whip out for the next ten races.

'My first ever winner over jumps came at Chepstow when Articeelagh obliged. Here again there was only a neck to spare in this novice hurdle and I thought I had done very well, holding him up and then coming with a late run. I was delighted that I had just pipped the second after a hectic battle up the straight. I thought I was Josh Gifford the Second. It was only later that I discovered I had not been so clever. The rider of the second horse (Sunarise, who later became a top point-to-pointer) was such a non-trier he was warned off. But Frenchie loved to share the enjoyment. He was, and still is, a different class to other trainers trying to do well with apprentices. He is not too grand to share the success of his youngsters.'

Scott, who gained the best of his 100 wins on Henry Alper's Persian Empire in the Imperial Cup, retired from riding in March, 1970 when he suffered two bad injuries to his back. He rides out occasionally and when he officially took over from Roger Mortimer at the *Sunday Times* produced a complete scoop when he rode Red Rum in a gallop prior to the 1975 Grand National while less athletic scribes could only describe the events at high tide at the now famous Southport sands.

Another star ex-pupil of the famous Frenchie Nicholson riding academy is Tony Murray, now first jockey to Ryan Price at Findon. He has all the trade marks of an apprentice who has learnt his art with the careful tuition of Nicholson. Perfectly mannered at all times he is a shining example of how Frenchie's magical ways with kids transforms then from starry-eyed apprentices into fully matured horsemen. As with Pat Eddery, Murray was bred for the job.

Later in Murray's career when he was 'jocked off' Giacometti, he said: 'I went and saw my old guv'nor and asked him what he thought. If it had not been for Mr Nicholson's advice I think I might have packed in the job and that would not have been a wise move. He gave me some wonderful advice and I am glad I listened to him.'

The Murray-St George situation was highlighted before the 1975 Derby when Lester Piggott was booked as the big race jockey for Bruni after the grey had been beaten with Tony on board at Goodwood. Joked Tony: 'I suppose everybody has a cross to bear and mine is the cross of St George.'

This is sad really but racing is big business. Charles St George has often quoted me his answer to all these 'jockeying off' criticisms. He says with complete candour: 'If you had a horse in a big race you would want the best jockey in the world – and that's Lester Piggott. What can possibly be wrong with wanting the best?' It is hard to disagree but it has been tough on Murray, especially as he rode such a brilliant race to land the Oaks for the St George camp on Ginevra. There was no criticism of Murray's handling of that delicate filly, who had to be coaxed along and held up for a late run. She was later sold to Japan for 106 000 guineas to shatter the existing Newmarket Sales record at that time. Not only has Nicholson produced a top-class rider in Murray, with a very likable and happy outlook on life, but he also stepped in at a difficult time with some golden words of advice. But for Frenchie's advice, Murray could have quit and missed the runaway win on Bruni in the 1975 St Leger, and later a highly creditable seventh in the Prix de l'Arc de Triomphe.

Another youngster who has made his mark in racing is Roger Wernham. Says Frenchie: 'He simply wrote to me for a job and I took him on. He has gone from strength to strength.' Ironically it was Peter O'Sullevan, the unrivalled king of commentators and much-respected racing journalist, who played a big part in Wernham's successful career. It was on Peter's fabulously game little front runner Attivo that Wernhan really hit the headlines. But it could have been a different lad who stole the glory but for Nicholson. Explains Peter: 'I have always favoured putting up boys in races on my horses. They don't hurt a horse. I think success in racing is more fun if it is done as a team. Racing has got to be fun. If a horse and a kid are successful together then it helps everybody. Often a horse can make an apprentice.

'Attivo had been ridden by Frenchie's youngster Chris Leonard and by Harry Ballantine. Then because my trainer Cyril Mitchell was friendly with Ted Smyth we also put up Alan Bond, who impressed me greatly. But at the start of Attivo's three-year-old career Leonard had lost his allowance and I had to think of getting another boy to ride him. After Attivo had won the *Daily Express* Triumph Hurdle I told Frenchie: "I shall be after another of your boys to ride him on the Flat next season." The memory of the youngster Richard Fox riding at Windsor stuck in my mind and I was keen to get him. But Frenchie answered: "Not that one just yet. I think I have just the boy for you in Roger Wernham." ' Nicholson's advice yet again proved to be ideal for Attivo went on to win the Ladbroke Chester Cup by a short head from Kambalda and then the Joe Coral Northumberland Plate. The only time Wernham failed to score on Attivo in 1974 was when they finished fifth behind Inventory in the Joe Coral Newbury Autumn Cup. But from his three hurdle wins and two wins with Wernham aboard on the Flat – he won his first five races of the year – O'Sullevan won £26521 in prize money. And that does not include the winning bets, as ice-cool Peter remains one of the shrewdest punters ever to take 10–1 about a 6–1 shot. Yet amazingly Peter would willingly have sold Attivo for £1000 at the end of his two-year-old career.

Recalls Peter: 'He ran five times as a two-year-old and certainly was no world-beater. There was nothing to do but keep him in training but there seemed little prospect of success. One of Cyril Mitchell's owners took a bit of a fancy to him and Cyril asked me whether I would be willing to part with him. I said I would be prepared to let him go but only if he remained in the stable. I said "I want £1000 for him" but Cyril said "I could not really recommend him at that price" so I kept him. When he ran his first race as a three-year-old at Doncaster he was well fancied. I had lost so much money on him the previous year in a race at Newmarket when he was ridden by Brian Jago that I thought I should have a little crack and had £1000 to £140 but again he disappointed. He had worked well before the race but Geoff Lewis said that he could not ride one side of him. I was having dinner with Geoff shortly afterwards and was joking: "I shall have to get a kid to ride him as you obviously can't." We laughed but he did give me some encouragement by saying: "If I were you I would not condemn him too quickly. I can't put it into words but I reckon there is something there." ' Lewis was dead right and after Attivo had touched off Kambalda by a whisker at Chester many a happy pressman woke up the next day with a thick head after the celebrations. Attivo's performances saw Peter O'Sullevan voted the Owner of the Year by the Horserace Writers and Reporters Association but this had nothing to do with the imbibing Chester press-room voters! Typically modest Peter was almost embarrassed by the award but the wildly delighted reception both he and little Attivo got in the winners' enclosure at Chester and Cheltenham clearly showed what popular winners they were. Mention, of course, besides Wernham must also be made of Cyril Mitchell, the now retired Epsom trainer who did so much to transform Attivo from an unsuccessful selling-plater into such a lion-hearted trier. Picture Peter waiting almost shyly for Attivo to be led into the winners' unsaddling position at the jam-packed Cheltenham Festival and it is easy to think that this was just another winner for the smartly groomed commentator whose tones have become known to millions on television as he rattles off the horses in running as quickly, and accurately, as a highly skilled auctioneer. But big race ownership success has not always walked hand in hand with O'Sullevan.

It was back in 1939 when Peter's uncle sent him a chaser who was reputed to be a half-brother to the Gold Cup winner Morse Code. Peter told me: 'I was living in a small flat in Chelsea at the time and begged my uncle to let me have the horse rather than have him put down because of the war. One morning there was a knock on my door and the horse, Wild Thyme II, had arrived. Every time I drive over Putney Bridge I recall the day I rode the old hunter over the bridge and down to Richmond Park. Full livery at that time cost three pounds but I could not afford that so I had him on half livery at thirty bob a week.

'Because of the war they were digging trenches in Richmond Park. I used to jump Wild Thyme II over the trenches. He used to go like the wind and I was convinced that I had a certain Gold Cup winner. At that time I did not really know anybody in racing and was a silver ring punter. But I knew of a trainer my stepfather had dealings with. When I rang he had joined up for the war but his head lad, Charlie Bell, had taken over. I told him that I had this truly fantastic horse which went like lightning in Richmond Park. When I cycled on my bike down to Epsom, Bell, a great character, told me: "All horses gallop fast past trees." Anyway Bell told me that it would cost £4 a week to keep the horse in training and I told him that I could only afford to keep him in training for six weeks to two months at the very outside. I used to ride him out at gallops, or rather he would take me along as he had a very strong hold. We entered him up for Cheltenham and everything was going fine until I had a letter from my uncle saying that he had not sent me the half-brother to Morse Code but an old hunter and he trusted that I would not try and turn him into a racehorse. I immediately tore down on my bike to Epsom but Charlie was marvellous about my mistake. So he ran his first race saying in the formbook that the dam's pedigree was unknown. When he was due to run for the third time at Plumpton on February 22nd, 1941 his usual jockey was injured so I planned to ride him. Trying to lose a lot of weight I contracted pneumonia on the eve of the race and could not ride. Charlie arranged for Frenchie Nicholson, then one of the top jockeys, to take over instead. Although I was ill I went down to Plumpton. Frenchie pulled up Wild Thyme II after he had completed the first circuit but he was just about to be lapped by the leaders. But I can remember the head lad Wally Green dashed down and shouting all kinds of abuse at Frenchie. He said "He would have pissed in. Whey did you pull him up? He was just about to get going." It was the first time I saw the unique optimism of racing which everybody needs at one time or another to sustain them.'

O'Sullevan then concentrated on leasing horses he had bought for £50 to £100. He had to wait fifteen agonizing years before he finally had his first winner, which was Pretty Fair at Windsor on March 11th, 1954. His first Flat winner was Just Friendly at Lincoln on March 24th, 1958. So Peter waited a long time for his much deserved success with Be

Friendly, who won £43880 from his twelve sprint race successes and ten places. Until Wernham and Attivo came on the scene Peter rated Be Friendly's success in the 1966 Vernon's Sprint Cup at Haydock as his happiest racing experience but now he has several to choose from. Peter's great love in his early days was greyhound racing. Many is the time he has dashed back from Edinburgh to be able to back the 'good thing' in the last at White City dog track. He recalls: 'Charlie Bell and I used to go flapping at places like Newmarket. My only form of transport was a motor bike and sidecar. Charlie used to sit in the sidecar with the greyhound on his knee. We used to have to stop the bike every so often so that he could have a little exercise. I used to be so keen on greyhounds that after watching the Irish Derby at the Curragh on the Saturday I used to fly back to London for the Greyhound Derby at the White City before going over to France on the Sunday – three Derbys in two days!' Peter now purrs to the races in the latest Jag – a far cry from the sidecar days.

He is full of praise for the Nicholsons – 'you must talk of Frenchie and Diane in the same breath' – and the way they have taught their youngsters. 'Frenchie says that he can't teach them to ride – only to steer. But that can't be true when you think of the great success he has had with his boys. They both work so hard and do everything for the boys. They teach them all the qualities and are especially keen that they learn to be articulate when out of the saddle. It's all so important. If anybody wants a boy to ride for them Frenchie and Diane will drive halfway across the world just to sit him in the saddle.'

Cook, Murray, Eddery and Wernham. The Nicholson flair of producing top class apprentices, who have since turned into fully fledged riders in their own right, was bound to continue. And the sequence was kept rolling along the day a carrot-topped youngster called Richard Fox arrived from Ireland to join the now famous Cheltenham academy of riding. Like Eddery he had done his homework with Seamus McGrath in Ireland. Now he had joined the Nicholson school to finalize his junior career.

Fox came from McGrath but like Roger Wernham it was simply a letter to Nicholson which gave Ian Johnson his chance in racing. He soon showed that he, too, had all the right qualities and the highly talented Whatcombe trainer Arthur Budgett was quick to spot his potential. So highly was Johnson rated by Budgett that he was specially retained to ride Budgett's 1975 2,000 Guineas and Derby colt, Dominion.

Nicholson possesses all the well-known Yorkshire qualities and it is hardly surprising that when it comes to cricket his favourite characters are Brian Close and Ray Illingworth. These two England players have the same kind of rugged determination that Nicholson has succeeded on.

At Newbury one day, in the spring of 1975, before the opening race, which was an apprentices' contest, Nicholson and I chatted about his youngsters. Royal trainer Ian Balding approached and said: 'I suppose you have about half the jockeys in this race.' Nicholson chuckled merrily. The idea of turning out so many of the youngsters in one race certainly appealed to him. He said: 'You know, the other day all six boys in my yard were out riding somewhere or other. I had to do the evening stables myself but I didn't mind. The biggest thrill of my life was seeing Tony Murray winning the Oaks on Ginevra. Then Pat won the Derby on Grundy and that was an even bigger thrill. Frankly I can't make a living out of training horses but I can out of these boys.' And with another friendly smile he added: 'They are good lads. Good lads. Every single one of them.' Nobody can argue with that for the Nicholson record is truly remarkable.

4. 'The boy did everything right'

Tim Molony was a happy man as he sped north to Liverpool from his stables at Wymondham, near Melton Mowbray in Leicestershire on March 30th, 1968. All was well for the former National Hunt champion jockey as he set out for the Flat meeting at Aintree on the Friday before the Grand National. On the Thursday Molony had produced a winner when Go To Work had won the Thursby Selling Plate for two-year-olds by 2½ lengths. After Geoff Lewis had steered Go To Work home Molony was pleased to see the bidding race up to 900 guineas before he was sold to the Irish Bloodstock Agency. Now as he journeyed to Liverpool Molony's mind flashed ahead to two other runners. But no matter how much he dreamed ahead Molony could not possibly have guessed the triumphs that lay in store for a horse and an apprentice he was to see perform that day. For he was to saddle up an almost unknown three-year-old ridden by Lester Piggott and give a ride to an equally unknown apprentice, who had never ridden in a race on English soil before. The moderately rated three-year-old was Red Rum and the young jockey was Pat Eddery, who only twelve days previously had celebrated his sixteenth birthday.

Ruddy-faced Molony takes up the story of how he was the first trainer in England to give Eddery the leg-up in a racecourse parade ring. The brilliant ex-jump jockey, who rode over 900 winners including four consecutive Champion Hurdles, said: 'I had this three-year-old filly called Dido's Dowry. She was a good little filly who I picked up for only 300 quid at Newmarket Sales. She won twice as a two-year-old from six outings. When I entered her for the Hylton

Handicap Stakes at Liverpool she got only 6 st 8 lb in the handicap.

'I couldn't use any of the top riders and had to start thinking about fixing up one of the smart young apprentices. To be honest I tried to get a couple of lads but it did not materialize. Then I remembered that Frenchie Nicholson always had the odd boy or two knocking about. I rode against Frenchie over jumps and he was a truly great jockey. When I rang him up and said I wanted a boy to ride Dido's Dowry at Aintree he said he had a youngster and that I would know the name. When he said "Patrick Eddery" I knew that he must be referring to a son of Jimmy Eddery, the old jockey who I had ridden against in a few hurdle races in Ireland.

'Frenchie said that he was a good lad and that was enough for me. He would be the last person to recommend a young lad who turned out to be a failure. Eddery was engaged to ride the filly and I can remember Frenchie telling me at the course before the race that although this was the lad's first ride since he came over from Ireland he could possibly turn out to be a good 'un. Frenchie took the kid, he looked very small and frail in those days, and showed him all round the course. It was only a six furlong race but Frenchie left nothing to chance and the kid must have known every blade of grass at Aintree and every running rail by the time they came back. I had never met young Pat before but he impressed me straight away as being a very well mannered chap.'

If Pat Eddery had ridden a novice chaser in the Grand National he could not have had a more eventful ride than Dido's Dowry. For, like many a jockey at Aintree, Eddery was to end up fairly and squarely on his backside in his first ever race in England. And this was a Flat race! Says Pat: 'I was told that she was quite a lively filly and that she could get rather excited. She was perfect in the paddock and on the way down to the start. The size of Aintree rather overawed me but I did not feel as nervous as I thought I would do. Then when we lined up at the start for the old barrier start everything suddenly seemed to go wrong. The filly got excited – I was probably a little excited too – and when another horse, Morning Service charged the tapes she followed suit and off we went together. Having clobbered the tapes I was thrown off. Luckily she was captured pretty quickly and not too much damage was done. But I can remember thinking what a terrible start it was.'

Says Molony: 'Dido's Dowry was just a little keen and flew off with him. But after the inital setback they quickly reunited and Pat gave her a good race and finished sixth, not all that far behind the fourth and fifth. Of course it was very early to forecast how Pat was going to do as a jockey but he certainly did little wrong in the race and I was well pleased with his performance.' Dido's Dowry, who was a 20–1 outsider, was sixth behind the Atty Corbett-trained Alpine.

Eddery's first ride in public in England – and only the second in his career – was really a dramatic race besides the two runners charging the tapes and unseating their riders. For Derreen was backed down to 5–2 favourite after opening at much longer odds. But the five-year-old stumbled in the race and Lester Piggott fell. So Eddery's debut race in England was a really unusual affair. Molony, who won the Champion Hurdle on Hatton's Grace in 1951 and followed up with a hat-trick on Sir Ken in successive years at Cheltenham, said: 'Eddery was very excited about the whole race but kept a cool head during the actual running of the race. I can see him now coming into the paddock for the first time wearing the red and green colours of Dido's Dowry's owner Bob Day, who used to farm near Northampton.'

Apart from winning the seller on the Thursday and giving Eddery his first ride in England on the Friday, Molony also had another reason to be pleased. For an hour after Eddery had ridden Dido's Dowry Tim saw his Red Rum run a really good race to finish second to Alan's Pet in the Earl of Sefton's Handicap Stakes.

Eddery says: 'I think it was the fact that Lester Piggott was in the same race which really impressed me. I used to dream all the time that one day I would be champion jockey and ride a Derby winner but I never really thought that I would one day line up before a race with Lester there. He was always my idol as a youngster, although Bill Williamson was a man who I tried to style myself on. Since then I have come to admire jockeys like Willie Carson, Geoff Lewis and Tony Murray, and I have always thought that Greville Starkey is one of the most under-rated of the current jockeys.' The day after Eddery and Red Rum appeared on the Liverpool card it was Brian Fletcher, later to be associated with Red Rum, who stole the glory when he won the Grand National on Red Alligator. But Pat was not there to see the northern horse triumph. After his ride on Dido's Dowry it was back to Cheltenham, Frenchie Nicholson doing the chauffeuring. Says Pat: 'In those days I got ten bob a week. I used to like going to the movies but if I had spent my money on sweets I would have to go through the week without seeing a film. The night after my first race in England it was straight back to the dormitory.'

Dido's Dowry, who was a tiny little filly, went on to have nine more races that season. She then went to stud and has since bred a couple of winners. Eddery had his moment of worry with Dido's Dowry but he impressed Molony. Nicholson looks back: 'The boy did everything right and did not panic when he got thrown off. I was pleased with him.' The filly showed that she was a lively customer later that summer. Running at Beverley in June she bolted with Ernie Johnson on her back and completed an entire circuit of the course before he could control her. In her next race at Kempton she was ridden by George Duffield and this proved a winning combination at 11–2. Eddery started off in England with Molony but strangely he has had very few rides for him since. 'Several times I have contacted Frenchie or even spoken to Pat himself but he has either been fixed up in the race I want him for or he is off at another meeting,' related Tim sadly.

'Having had one ride I must admit that I was desperately keen to get into the full swing of the game,' recalls Pat. But Frenchie Nicholson is not the kind of man who would rush an apprentice into racing. Eddery Jnr had obvious talents but he still had to have the full education and grooming needed to turn him into a jockey who would one day be a champion and be talked about in the same breath as the legendary Lester Piggott.

Having had his first race at the controversial Aintree racecourse, which seems to attract owners of the track who have a rare eye for making the headlines, it was Warwick where Pat was next seen in action. On April 15th he partnered 20–1 outsider Cleodora in the Last Straw Selling Handicap. On this moderate six-year-old, trained by Frenchie Nicholson himself, Pat finished eleventh. Kushi, the winner, was trained by Bruce Hobbs and owned by Mrs Laurette Baerlein, wife of Richard, the well-known *Observer* and *Guardian* racing correspondent. Later in April Pat took part in the Compton Stakes at Newbury when riding the aptly named Irishman. This race was good experience in itself as no fewer than forty-two runners took part. The winner was 33–1 outsider Mustwyn, trained by Ryan Price. Says Pat: 'In those early days I was not riding outstanding horses but I was gaining experience.' A long car ride to Ripon was next on the cards for Pat when he rode Real Star in the Hackfall Apprentice Handicap on April 24th. Ironically Pat, who finished tenth, came in just one place behind a filly he had ridden earlier that month – Dido's Dowry.

There was a touch of irony about Pat's next ride, which turned out to be the first time ever he was seen to finish in the frame. Riding the eight-year-old gelding March Fast, Pat finished third in the Empire Handicap at Bath on May 23rd. The winner of the one mile five furlong race was Prince Taffy, ridden by Duncan Keith and trained by Peter Walwyn. Four years later in 1972 it was to be Eddery who stepped in for the plum Walwyn job when Duncan Keith was forced to quit after years of wasting had seriously affected his health. When Eddery again finished third on March Fast in the Apprentice Handicap at Chepstow on June 4th he was spotted by racing journalists as a good prospect. 'This young son of the former Irish champion jockey Jimmy Eddery has a great chance of making the grade as a rider,' glowed one favourable report at the time. Further rides were given by Nicholson to Eddery and trainer Frank Freeman was one handler who quickly spotted Pat's potential. He gave Eddery the first of his many seconds, before his initial winner, when he partnered Tecilyn to be second in the Malmesbury Handicap at Bath on July 18th. There was only a length in the winning margin of Welsh Bede, who was ridden by Taffy Thomas and trained by one of the most amusing personalities in racing, Doug Marks. It is interesting to note that many of the apprentices who took part in races in which Pat rode are no longer in racing today. So many good boys burst onto the scene and earn good reports but there is a high percentage who have one or two rides and are never heard of again. As if to celebrate the first time that he had more than one ride in a day Pat followed Tecilyn's second with a third on Royal Sport in the very next event, the Dunkirk Handicap. Here he finished only a head and three quarters of a length behind Bobby Elliott on Golden Beaker and Joe Mercer on Night Lot. The sixteen-year-old was mixing with the men and performing well. Says Pat: 'I did okay but had a lot of rides and was getting worried about when I would finally break my duck and ride a winner. It seemed to be one short head and neck after another at one time but I never thought of packing it in. I loved working with horses and was sure that racing was going to be my life.'

When Pat finished well down the field on Alex M in the Russell Nursery Handicap at Windsor on October 5th it was his last race of the 1968 campaign. Alex M had won his previous race for Frenchie Nicholson when Brian Jago came home easily by four lengths to win a seller at Bath in August. The two-year-old was owned by Diane Nicholson. With just over twenty rides in his first season Eddery made a quiet but confident start to his racing career. Getting beaten by small margins frustrated Pat but he kept about his job well. Says Jimmy Eddery: 'I can remember Pat saying that he thought he would never actually win a race. But I told him that was how everybody felt like to start with. I tried to impress upon him that in racing there is only one way to be successful and that's by hard work. I know that he got the message.'

It was the 1969 Flat season which saw Pat Eddery emerge as one of the best apprentices in the land. Frenchie Nicholson recommended him to many trainers and those who heeded to the advice were certainly glad of his services. Although still inexperienced when it came to the number of rides, Eddery showed a remarkable and mature flair in the saddle. He had to wait for his first ever winner until the Epsom Spring meeting of 1969, but once he had broken his duck the winners started to flow in nicely. Not a raging torrent of success – what could you expect from a kid of only seventeen? – but a slow, steady stream of winners. It was trainer Michael Pope who put Pat on the winning way and because Alvaro was such an interesting horse I have dealt with him separately. Alvaro gave Pat his first winner on April 24th but by the end of the season Pat had ridden twenty-three winners and had shot up the apprentices table to be only fourth from the top behind Clive Eccleston, who had forty-one successes. Champion apprentices come and go like the tide but happily Eccleston is one promising youngster who did go on to make the grade, although his score when champion apprentice still remains the best total he has ever attained for one season.

Michael Pope realized Eddery's tremendous potential probably quicker that any other trainer, with the obvious exception of Frenchie Nicholson, who always gave the quiet-spoken young Irishman star billing. Of Pat's twenty-three winners in 1969 nine were for the Streatley trainer. Next on the list in order of winners was Brian Swift, with three, while Lambourn trainer Freddie Maxwell produced two winners for Eddery in 1969. Staff Ingham and Ryan Price also contributed two successes. Getting Eddery more firmly known in racing by giving him a winning ride that year were Jeremy Tree, Doug Smith, Richmond Sturdy, Herbert Jones and Frank Freeman, who was based near to Frenchie's yard in Cheltenham.

The courses where Pat rode winners in 1969 were Epsom (four), Newmarket, Kempton, Salisbury, Alexandra Park, Doncaster (two), Brighton, Royal Ascot, Ascot, Sandown (four), Newcastle, Redcar, Folkestone, Bath, York and Newbury. Pat's winnings for his owners that season amounted to over £20000 so there was already gathering quite a little nest egg for him, safely kept by Frenchie Nicholson, until

44

he came out of his apprenticeship. By the end of the season he had emerged as one of the top up-and-coming jockeys and shrewd judges were already noting his name.

The only incident to take place in the first two years which caused any alarm was at Warwick on July 27th, 1968 when Pat was riding a three-year-old filly called Mayella in the Packwood Handicap over seven furlongs. Four furlongs from home Eddery was brought down when Tudor Sun fell. Much Love was also brought down in what appeared to be a nasty three-horse pile-up. But Eddery enjoyed the second miracle escape of his young life and simply suffered a minor knee injury.

When it comes to smart trainers – men who achieve great success with a small string of horses – it would be hard to find an equal to Epsom-based Staff Ingham. In a good career as a jockey he rode on the Flat from 1922 to 1925, winning the Royal Hunt Cup and the Irish 2,000 Guineas. Then he switched to the Jumping game and rode under National Hunt rules from 1927 to 1939, winning amongst many other big races the Imperial Cup. Like Nicholson he was a Wootton pupil. Whereas Nicholson made his name as a fear-nothing chase rider, Ingham was regarded as the ideal man to ride over hurdles. When he switched to training in 1939 he again joined the top bracket – not so much in numbers of winners, as he has never had a large string. But many an Ingham winner has roared in and left the bookmakers without a single smile on their faces. His almost yearly haul of winning two-year-olds at Epsom is a wonderful feat in itself and has been much appreciated by punters not afraid to lay out large sums of money at short odds. In 1969 Staff had a horse who was an ideal ride for a boy. Staff had a good youngster in the then nineteen-year-old Chris Dwyer, who had won twice on Baletta and Medina Boy and once on Palyana. He was a good seven pound claimer but when Ingham and Nicholson met at the races Frenchie was continually mentioning that he thought he had a youngster who was a little bit out of the ordinary.

Staff Ingham is a shrewd man in racing but there are few more knowledgeable and consistently correct men in their predictions than the great Phil Bull. *Timeform* overlord since 1947, the whiskery faced Halifax supremo has made a fortune out of fearlessly backing his judgements over the years. Of course, on occasions he has been wrong but his record as a gambler over the years is second to none. It is not surprising that he had horses in training with Ingham. Over the years Bull, a truly remarkable man in many ways, has bred and owned some wonderful racehorses. Orgoglio won the Champagne Stakes and the Victoria Cup; Eubulides (Chesham Stakes and Richmond Stakes); Arietta (Craven Stakes and third in the 1,000 Guineas); Dionisio (Victoria Cup and Wokingham Stakes); Anadem (Great Surrey Foal Stakes); and Orinthia (Jubilee Handicap and Manchester Cup). Besides these winners he also sold Romulus as a foal before he went on to win many races including the Greenham Stakes, Sussex Stakes, Queen Elizabeth II Stakes, Prix du Moulin at Longchamp and second in the 2,000 Guineas. Perhaps the best day's work Bull ever did was when he bought Orieene for £250 at a public auction. She was the dam of his good horses Orgoglio, Orinthia, Orycida, Orarca, Ocarienne, Orinda, Orbaneja, Oroondates and Orsillus. It is the mare Orinthia who becomes involved in the Eddery story.

In 1966 Phil Bull sent Orinthia to Never Say Die, the 1954 Derby winner who gave Lester Piggott his first Epsom Classic victory. The result was Philoctetes, who was to feature prominently in Pat's early big race days.

Bull, who gained a B.Sc. at Leeds University and could have been a maths genius if he had not turned his thoughts to racing, happily recalled Philoctetes' career. Bull told me how he had noticed a young apprentice in action. 'There was no fluke about how Pat Eddery rode the horse. He was a bloody good rider even in those days. I had seen him several times and liked him.' Bull went on to tell me that he will never forget the first time Philoctetes raced as a three-year-old, back in 1967 and before Eddery teamed up with him in 1969. 'I suppose it was one of the biggest bets of my life,' recalls Bull, whose *Timeform* charity meetings have been superb ventures bringing in over £200000 mainly for the

National Society for Cancer Relief. 'Philoctetes' first race as a three-year-old was at Yarmouth and judged by the way he was going at home and everything else he was the certainty of the century – or so I thought. I had a couple of runners at Pontefract that day and did not go to Yarmouth. But he got beaten and finished behind horses he would have given two stone and a beating to later on in his career.'

In fact Philoctetes did little in his two and three-year-old career to suggest that he was going to be a big money-spinner for Phil Bull. But all changed when he reached four years old. He won his first race in 1968 when taking the Charles Elsey Memorial Challenge Trophy at Beverley on April 27th by two lengths from First Phrase. That day he was ridden by Peter Robinson (who later switched to training successfully at Newmarket) and was trained by Teddy Lambton. His starting price of 6–5 suggests that his *Timeform* rating must have given him something of a good chance. His next win gave Phil great satisfaction because he won the *Timeform* 21st Anniversary Cup at Redcar on May 4th, when he defied a seven pound penalty but still had 1½ lengths to spare over Zardia. He was again ridden by Peter Robinson. Geoff Oldroyd rode Philoctetes next when third in the Jack Woolf Cup behind The Accuser at Wolverhampton on July 20th but Robinson was back on board when he finished tenth in the George Atkins Gold Cup at Nottingham on August 12th. Peter also rode him in his next outing, the Tote Investors Trophy Handicap at Ripon on August 17th.

From here Robinson went on to win on him in the W.D. & H.O. Wills Trophy at Newcastle on September 2nd and five days later, defying a five pound penalty, he won the Hambleton Cup at Thirsk by an easy five lengths from Colditz Story. He had one more win that season when he took the Eglinton and Winton Memorial Handicap at Ayr on September 8th where he showed his real class by lumping an eight pound penalty to victory. But it was a year later that Eddery became involved in the Philoctetes story.

Staff Ingham now had Philoctetes and after two un-placed runs he saddled him to win the Greenhall Whitley Gold Trophy at Chester on July 19th. This gave Philoctetes an eight pound penalty in the £5614 Vaux Gold Tankard at Redcar on July 30th and so Ingham wisely looked round for a useful young apprentice who could get a few pounds off the handicap and added penalty weight. Having spoken to Frenchie Nicholson many times and heard the name 'Eddery' mentioned regularly it was not surprising that he contacted the Cheltenham trainer and booked the young Irishman for the ride. Eleven runners took part in the race but Eddery led them all a merry dance and for the first time in his career rode a winning waiting race from the front. He took the lead after just one furlong of the one mile six furlong trip and then quickened in the last two furlongs and went clear by four lengths to win from Avast, also a previous winner, with Sea Robber four lengths away third. Recalls Phil: 'Pat rode him with a lot of confidence and showed even at that stage of his career that he had the potential to be a very fine jockey.' Pat can remember little of the race but admits: 'I know I followed my instructions and could hardly believe how easily we won.'

Pat was again on Philoctetes when he ran in the Johnnie Walker Ebor Handicap at the big York meeting on August 20th. Again he led after one furlong and was indeed second coming into the straight but soon weakened and finished well down the field behind the shock 40–1 winner, Big Hat, trained by Dave Hanley. That was the end of Philoctetes' campaign for 1969. Thanks to Alvaro (twice), Singing Girl and Sky Rocket, Eddery had four times previously won races over £1000 but the Vaux Gold Tankard win was the first success he had registered over £5000. It was not to be the last by a long, long way and Philoctetes was again to prove a useful ally.

Philoctetes was indeed a good servant for Phil Bull. 'He won as many as eight trophy races for me,' recalls Phil, who sold him to stud at the end of his career and is now in New Zealand. His sire, Never Say Die, stood at the National Stud at Newmarket until his death in the autumn of 1975 and here again racing proves a very much interwoven story because there is an Eddery tie-up. For when Grundy ended his racing days he, too, went to the National Stud and made it three Derby winners on the premises; the 1969 Epsom hero Blakeney is also one of the distinguished inmates as is the unforgettable 1971 scorer Mill Reef. While the Levy Board has to fork out about £750000 to keep Grundy in England, Never Say Die did not cost the National Stud a penny as he was a gift from his American owner Robert Sterling Clark. The only reservation Clark stipulated was that Never Say Die should be available annually to ten Irish mares. In 1962 Never Say Die achieved rare fame when his own son Larkspur won the Derby.

Precious few Derby winners have actually sired a winning Derby son. But in 1975 it did look well on the cards as Green Dancer, son of the Triple Crown hero Nijinsky, appeared to have a great chance. Nijinsky beat the French-trained Gyr when he won the Derby in 1970 and he, too, had a son in the race in Harry Wragg's Hobnob. But history did not repeat itself and Green Dancer, although a red-hot favourite finished sixth and Hobnob only beat two of the eighteen runners. Last place was predictably taken throughout by the horse who was 5–1 favourite to trail in behind the others . . . Tanzor, ironically another son of Nijinsky. Green Dancer appeared capable of putting Nijinsky alongside Never Say Die in the achievement of siring a Derby winner. But then along came a remarkable horse called Grundy and an equally remarkable jockey called Eddery and a different story will go into the racing archives.

5. The Amazing Alvaro

'Never bloody well heard of him,' came the almost un-interested reply from Berkshire trainer Major Michael Pope when his wife Kay returned home from an afternoon's jump racing at nearby Newbury early in the Spring of 1969. The master of Wood Farm stables at Streatley showed only mild interest as his wife went on to describe an ordinary day at the sports. But this was no routine trip, for it was to bring together an experienced and much respected trainer with an unknown apprentice jockey called Pat Eddery and a quite remarkable horse called Alvaro, at this time still a maiden after nine unsuccessful races on the Flat as a two and three-year-old in 1967 and 1968.

It is often horses who make men rather than men who make horses. Virtually every trainer or jockey, who has progressed to the top in racing, can look back and name one horse who started the bonanza. With Eddery it was the bay colt Alvaro.

One wonders if Ryan Price would have set out on his fabulously successful career if he had not 'had a touch' with a thirteen-year-old maiden at Plumpton the first time he really put the money down. On one of my visits to Findon Price affectionately stroked his favourites – Grand National winner Kilmore, Cesarewitch winner Persian Lancer, Schweppes winner Le Vermontois and his wife Dorothy's faithful servant Charlie Worcester. Also in this veteran group is Gold Cup winner What a Myth. 'It's horses like these who have made me,' he boomed in typical style. 'Without them the public would never have heard of me. They would have raced to within an inch of their life for me.'

Price's first ever winner at Plumpton came with the same horse he had previously planned to win with at Wye. Ironically a flint broke the fan belt of Price's car on the way to the races that day and he did not get there in time to declare him. But he later won at Plumpton and the Price success story was on the way. In those early days he admits: 'I didn't have enough money for a match box, let alone a horse box.'

All the young trainers today can thank one buy – often a lucky one – for putting them on the racing map, and attracting owners. Success makes for success and an ideal example is Lambourn trainer Barry Hills. But it was only the exploits of Frankincense and an ice-cool betting brain which started the ball rolling for Hills and enabled him to become firmly established with the 100-horse South Bank stables behind him. Ask him how a former apprentice jockey and then travelling head lad to John Oxley made the major transformation and he will quickly point to an oil painting above the fireplace in his lounge of the money-spinning Frankincense. Says Barry: 'In 1967 I simply could not see him getting beaten in the William Hill Gold Cup at Redcar. I backed him at 25–1 and picked up over £6000.' Nice work if you can get it but Hills was not yet finished with the bookmakers. The following year Frankincense won the Lincoln and this time Hills scooped a £9000 jackpot after backing him at 40–1. So it is easy to see how all trainers and jockeys have to have that initial bit of luck to put them on the way to fame – and in many cases fortune.

Eddery's lucky break came when Kay Pope decided to seek refuge from a shivery, snow-swept Newbury. In one of the crowded bars she bumped into Frenchie and Diane Nicholson and a chance conversation got under way. Recalls Kay: 'We were talking about the coming Flat season as two training families normally would.

'Frenchie said: "Does your old man want a good apprentice to ride for him next season? You may well laugh when I say this but I have a kid who has never been placed in over 50 races – hardly ever sighted. But he has the potential to be a very fine jockey and I just want him to get one or two opportunities. You may think I'm a right one to suggest him but when the season comes round and you want a good boy, remember the name . . . Pat Eddery." '

The message was delivered by Kay Pope when she returned home but one can hardly blame Michael for not getting over-excited. I visited Pope at his former yard before the start of the 1975 Flat season. Nestling in a hamlet in the valley of a 1 in 6 hill it is the most peaceful stable imaginable. Pope has now retired from training but still takes a more than active interest in the sport which was his life for thirty-five years. He is President of the National Trainers' Federation. He also manages the Dobsons Stud at Henley and the Hillfield Stud at Upper Basildon. It is the Dobsons Stud where his exceptional racehorse Birdbrook is now a stallion.

'Seems as though I was training for donkeys' years,' said Pope as he settled in his sun porch. 'I miss the training but I still manage a few for Lord Strathalmond and can go and see them on the gallops at Frank Cundell's place whenever I want to.

'I quite honestly had never heard of Patrick Eddery when my wife mentioned him to me way back in 1969. I probably would not have taken any more notice except that it was Frenchie Nicholson who praised the boy. If he says they are all right that's good enough for me. Let's face it – like Sam Armstrong used to be, he's become skilled at not only training horses but boys as well. It's a rare skill. No, if Frenchie says a boy has a good future and is 100 per cent okay then you can bet your life that this is the case. Tony Murray and Paul Cook both rode for me when they were with Frenchie. Bloody good boys both of them. Reliable and sensible apprentices. A young lad called Fred Messer used to ride for me as well but he became too heavy. He was another Nicholson special and once rode two winners for me on French Parade inside one week at Ascot.'

Pope, a ruddy faced man with a splendid sense of humour, talks with justifiable pride as he recalls how he gave Eddery the first winning chance. Dogs yap at his feet and a stern picture of Sir Winston Churchill gazes down as he relates how it was this seemingly moderate animal became Eddery's first winner and remains to this day one of his favourite horses.

'I went up to the horses-in-training sales at Newmarket to buy a few prospective jumpers. I wasn't really interested whether they turned out to be winners for me on the Flat or not. I did my homework and saw that Ian Balding had sent up this horse called Alvaro. He was bred by Ian's mother-in-law, Mrs Hastings Bass. I took a fancy to his breeding and decided that he would make a decent hurdler or jumper with any luck. I even rang up Paul Cook, who had ridden him a few times, and asked him what he thought of him. He told me: "He looks fine but has not really showed any form at all. I don't think that he is all that genuine." When I saw him he looked the part, although it did say on the catalogue that he was a wind-sucker. It's an odd habit some horses have and a horse is sometimes called a crib biter. Well, rightly or wrongly, I took a chance and bought him for 1800 guineas. At the same sales I also bought Sky Rocket for 3500 guineas and Tantalum. All were to go jumping but as it turned out only Tantalum took to this game and he won some good races for me, usually ridden by Frenchie Nicholson's son David. I thought I had made three good buys as I drove home from Newmarket. But I didn't think that for long.

'Late that night my head lad got hold of me to tell me that he had terrible problems loading Alvaro into his box after the sales. "Guv'nor, you have got a right bastard here. It took us about two hours to get him boxed up and we only managed it in the end by pushing him in backwards," ' Pope related. 'I thought that I had made a ricket and saw for myself. He was a queer old sort and when in the yard he would not go into his box unless he was steered in backwards. Still, we eventually got him in and went off to bed thinking that Alvaro was perhaps not such a good buy after all. In the middle of the night I knew for sure that he wasn't.

'God, you have never heard anything like it. He started wind-sucking and as his box was in the corner of the yard near to my house you could hear this terrible noise all night. He never stopped gripping his teeth on anything sticking out in his box and wind-sucking. I suppose it is a bit of a nervous complaint and could be compared with people who bite their nails. Quite frankly when horses start wind-sucking all they are doing is filling themselves with wind and the result is that all they do is pass wind all day! On the gallops Alvaro was worse than useless. He would gurgle away all night and wouldn't do a thing at exercise. I had to find a way of stopping the bugger wind-sucking or he would never have seen another racecourse in his life.

'Later on when I transformed him other trainers told me I must be a bloody magician. I never let on how I had done it because I always thought that he would make a good stallion and this business – if he went back to it – could have affected his sale price. But now that's all over and I can tell the secret of Alvaro . . . an electric wire. It was as simple as that.

'I decided to strip Alvaro's box completely. I took everything out and there was not a single item he could catch hold of to start wind-sucking. Horses can't do this if there is nothing for them to bite at. I then put an electric wire round the inside of his box. Of course, as he had nothing to grasp hold of he tried the wire and just got a sufficient enough electrical shock to make him back away. This could never really hurt him but it did make him think that it was not worth trying to play his old tricks again. I even took his loose manger out and he had to eat his grub off the floor. Amazingly my trick worked. From being a completely useless racehorse he soon started showing me on the gallops that he certainly had ability. I was delighted that everything had gone so well. Shortly before the start of the Flat season Alvaro was completely cured of this ghastly wind-sucking and was a different horse. By this stage I was beginning to think he would be an ideal ride for an amateur, or possibly an apprentice. And that's when I remembered that Frenchie Nicholson had mentioned one useful boy.

'I contacted Frenchie and met Patrick for the first time when he came down to ride Alvaro and other horses at work. From the very first time I ever watched him on a horse I knew he was a natural. You only had to see his hands to realize this. Even at the age of seventeen he rode and talked like a veteran. I really was most impressed and thought to myself how right Frenchie had been about the lad. On the gallops at home he always did everything he was told. Some lads are told to sit in behind the others but after they have gone a furlong they have charged off six lengths in front. Some horses simply run away with the lads but this never happened to Patrick.

'On April 11th Alvaro ran in the Gladiators Stakes over two miles at Ascot when he was ridden by that good amateur Bill O'Gorman. Christ! We must have had a fair bit on him that day as I see from my own records that he started 11–4 favourite. I can remember he was so well in at the weights that day and after what he had done on the gallops we had bombs on him. I can safely say that I have never seen a horse win any race so easily. The winning margin of one length could have been much, much greater. Mind you, it was not a very good race but we were clearly the best. I can remember O'Gorman saying to me after looking up the form that he thought his ride had no chance. But Alvaro roared in that day as though he was jet propelled. He simply pissed in. Of course, it was then that some of the other trainers asked me how I had performed such a miracle with him. Nobody knew the secret of the electric wire stopping him windsucking. Despite this win he was so well handicapped everywhere because I had got in as many entries as possible in a short time – I was certain he would win first time out for me.'

That day Bill O'Gorman was followed home by two well-known amateur riders – Philip Mitchell on Hornblue and Nick Gaselee on Publican. Also in the race were Gay Kindersley and Ben Leigh who subsequently became trainers.

Bill O'Gorman, who was only twenty-one when he steered Alvaro to his initial success, rode twelve winners as an amateur and four over hurdles as a professional before creating a record when he partnered Scarlet Wonder to victory in a seller at the first Newmarket meeting of 1975. For Bill was the first jockey-trainer to win at headquarters since the turn of the century. Based at the nearby Graham Place stables he went on a crash diet from early February and lost over two stone. He cut out alcohol completely and had only one meal a day in the evening – a frugal way of life that brings to mind another extremely weight-conscious Newmarket gentleman.

The stage was now set for Eddery to ride his first ever winner – ironically over the world-famous Derby trip at Epsom. Looking back he recalls: 'I lost count of how many rides I had before achieving the first success. I know that I got beaten in a couple of tight finishes early that season and at one stage was wondering when I would ever get off the mark. I was desperately keen to ride a winner but it never seemed to happen.'

Recalling Nicholson's sky-high praise for the young Irishman Pope contacted the Cheltenham-based trainer and arranged for Eddery to ride work for him. Eddery had two gallops on Alvaro before the big day came at Epsom on April 24th when he rode him in the Spring Apprentices' Handicap over 1½ miles. It was just thirteen days after O'Gorman's runaway win at Ascot but on this occasion thirteen was to prove a lucky number.

Flicking back through the pages of his private record book Pope immediately commented: 'He was 6–1 that day. What a good price! We stepped in again and had a bomb on him, although his jockey had never ridden a winner. That did not worry me for one minute. I had seen enough on the gallops to know that both horse and rider were capable of winning. When he stayed with us he slept in the lads' hostel with all the other boys. Most of them wanted to dart off to the nearest pub or cinema but not Patrick. Even at that age he wanted to sit and read the formbook. Often I found him all on his own weighing up the chances of his rides, while the others were out on the town. All he thought about was racing. When riding work he used his nut but I shall never forget the puzzled look he gave me when we stood in the parade ring at Epsom that day.

'He very soon asked: "How shall I ride him?" I looked down on him and said: "Just guide him, he'll win." To a kid who had been given several rides and never ridden a winner it must have sounded rather daft. He frowned a little and said: "Do you really mean that?" I suppose as a seven pound claimer who had never ridden a single winner it must have sounded rather peculiar advice.

'Of course it's history now how Alvaro skated in by three lengths. Pat was over the moon. But his first question was: "Where are you going to run him next?" Already he was thinking ahead. There is no doubt that the old electric wire had transformed his form and Alvaro had beaten the handicapper. Because of this win other trainers began to notice young Eddery and it helped that his father Jimmy Eddery was known as a top-class Irish jockey. All of a sudden the Nicholsons' phone started to buzz. But they were always very good to me. Out of loyalty they often turned down other rides for Patrick so that he could ride for me. One day he had the choice of four rides at Folkestone but they turned them all down so that I had first choice for him, although I only wanted him for one ride. That was typical of the Nicholsons. They always remembered that I had given him his first winner.

'After the Epsom race I was determined he should take his next opportunity and it came just six days later in the March Handicap over two miles at Newmarket. Looking at my file I see that he started at 100–30. Yet again I thought he was a good thing and backed him. He absolutely skated in by six lengths and everybody was very complimentary about the way I had improved his form. It was just a case of curing him from that wretched wind-sucking. To be perfectly frank, all he had done before was fart all over the place. He beat Lester Piggott into second place that day which especially pleased Pat.

'On May 8th Patrick again won on Alvaro in the Waldegrave Stakes over two miles at Kempton. The jolly old starting price was beginning to come down. He was only 2–1 that day but absolutely cantered in by eight lengths. In all these races Eddery was perfectly placed and did exactly as I told him. I never had a moment's worry with him and to this day I can't recall one race for me in which he did not ride totally to instructions. We were still beating the handicapper and Salisbury on May 15th was the next win in the 1¾ mile City Bowl Handicap. By now everybody knew that

Alvaro and this young jockey were a winning team and he started at 13–8 on but he won on his own by four lengths. On May 24th at Doncaster he not only won on Alvaro at 5–4 in the Harewood Handicap Stakes by two lengths but rode his first ever double when winning the opening race, the Arskey Handicap Stakes, for me on Pheidippides at 100–7. That horse was bred by Phil Bull.

'I still feel bloody proud that I gave him his first winner and his first double. Patrick had won five races on the trot on Alvaro in twenty-nine days and the horse had won six altogether in forty-two days. But it was time for the handicapper to clobber us.

'In the London Gold Cup at Ally Pally on June 10th Patrick and Alvaro should have won by ten minutes. But the track was too sharp and he was beaten a neck by John Gorton on Brightness. That evening he started at evens. When they were again beaten into second place by four lengths by Frankie Durr on Even Say in the Northumberland Plate at Newcastle on June 28th there were no excuses. We had enjoyed a great run with a horse who at the beginning of the season as a maiden four-year-old had been useless. After his wins he was very heavily handicapped and with his loss of form I decided to give him a breather. Later that summer David Nicholson took a string of horses over to Deauville and it was suggested that Alvaro should go. Patrick was booked up for rides in England and did not ride him. Anyway he had lost his form and he ran badly in two races when ridden by Paul Cook and Sandy Barclay. The old problem had returned. Without the magic electric wire he had started wind-sucking again like mad and he did not do himself justice. Yet again he would not travel anywhere unless he went in backwards. He had to be pushed backwards into his box and I understand that even when exercised in the sea at Deauville he would not go into the water unless he was backed in gently. He was a real character and I liked him a hell of a lot. But having lost so much of his form I decided that it was best to sell him as a stallion. He was sold privately to go to Australia and I was told he produced some fine foals. I don't suppose Patrick or I will forget him in a hurry.'

The first race on the Epsom card when Blakeney won the 1969 Derby saw Eddery win the Minora Handicap on Singing Girl for Brian Swift.

'By now Eddery was very much in demand. Few people realize what a great amount he owes to the Nicholsons, although Patrick is always the very first to say so. Diane Nicholson used to drive him hundreds of miles to race meetings. When it comes to producing apprentices the Nicholsons are in a class of their own. They not only taught him how to ride but were strict on how he should behave. I remember old Frenchie telling me: "Kick his backside if you have any trouble. If they are riding work the next morning be sure they don't have the price of a cinema ticket in their pocket!" Early to bed was one of the trademarks of the Nicholson boys. I remember one night a group of my lads and those of Frank Cundell were all going to the pictures. Patrick very much wanted to go but after he had scraped about in his pockets he found he did not have the money, so he had to stay in the hostel. It was a hard upbringing but has produced a most likable young man. Frenchie was always keen on perfect manners and would always clamp down quickly on any lads with remarks like "Take those hands out of your pockets".'

For Pope and Eddery 1969 was a good season. Between April 24th and September 30th the youngster rode nine winners for the stable and was placed twenty-five times. He was firmly establishing himself as a rider with top quality potential. Pope had given him the big lift-off and he was also to provide him with his first big race winner to put himself even more firmly in the public eye. And there can be no better place to attract attention than riding the winner of one of the major events at the glamour-filled Royal Ascot meeting.

Besides Alvaro, Pope had purchased Tantalum and Sky Rocket at the Newmarket horses-in-training sales. Eddery rode Tantalum a few times, and was placed on him but never won. He was bought as a potential jumper and adapted well to the obstacles. Alvaro, thanks to Pope's skilful handling and Eddery's teenage calmness, enjoyed a successful season, more than repaying the initial outlay. But if Pope thought that he had a prospective Champion hurdler in Sky Rocket he was in for a giant-sized shock.

Michael told me: 'Sam Armstrong trained him on the Flat and I thought he looked a good sort. Sam was a good friend of mine and he told me that Sky Rocket was absolutely sound. He had won two races in two seasons from fifteen starts. I liked him when I first saw him at Newmarket and was happy to get him for 3000 guineas. I had in mind a jumping career and did not think that he would do much on the Flat for me. I could not have been more wrong. He was a colty sort of horse. He hated the sight of hurdles and never jumped a single one for me. He would simply refuse or run out. I suppose being a colty type he was too frightened of hurting himself. He hated it so much I did not persevere. It was clear that he was never going to take to the jumping game.

'After Patrick had finished second on him to Raffingora in a boys' race at Ally Pally on April 21st I decided instead that the Wokingham Stakes at Royal Ascot would be his objective. I'm not saying that we fiddled with him but let's just say that when we won the Wokingham at 20–1 on June 20th with Patrick on board, it was not the biggest surprise of my life. It was not totally unexpected, you understand. My father, who owned Sky Rocket, loved a good bet and we had a fair old touch that day although there was a big field of twenty-one runners.

'By this stage of the summer Patrick was becoming very mature when it came to race riding. We would discuss how he would ride my horses and he played an active part in the talks. If I said something which he agreed with he would hardly say a word but I could tell the information was grinding round in his brain. If I said something which he clearly thought was cockeyed he would reply politely: "Do you really think so?" When he said that I knew that he did not think I was right. But he was never cocky.

'Before the Wokingham we both agreed that as he was drawn number one on the stand side it would be best if he jumped off and made all. I did have other ideas about how

60

he should ride the race at one time but he convinced me that this was the best policy and it worked a treat, he won by three quarters of a length. Even after gaining this first big race success Patrick was obviously overjoyed but there was never a hint of him becoming big-headed. He was a charming kid to talk to in front of owners. The Nicholsons' training had really worked with him.

'I never had to give Patrick a bollicking and in fact I have never given a jockey a bollicking in my life. Rather than have an awful barney I would rather not put the jockey up on the horse next time. They get the message that way. Patrick did have his spots of bother around this time but he never got into any trouble on any of my horses. He was young and determined to do well. I suppose he went for holes which simply were not there. Like Lester when he was young, the older jockeys did not like his enthusiasm all that much.

'Once or twice I had decent horses running and Patrick was at that time suspended. He had so much ambition, this lad, that it used to break his heart when listening to the results on the radio to learn that a horse he would have ridden had in fact won with another jockey on board. I used to say to him: "For Christ's sake cheer up. You will be back in a few days." If I had a winner he would have partnered but missed through a ban he was always the very first person to come up and say: "Well done."

'Right now he is at the top of his profession and I was delighted when he became champion. Some jockeys shoot to the top and then come down again but I don't think for a minute that this could happen to him. He has Peter Walwyn behind him and could not have a better man. He is also still very much under the eye of the Nicholsons and they give him the best possible advice. I remember one so-called wonder boy slipping backwards in his career. He was on the floor when I gave him a chance. He did nothing wrong but I told him point blank: "One slip and you needn't bother turning up the next day." Luckily it worked with this chap and he is still riding winners today.'

Eddery was lucky to have a man of Pope's wisdom and faith behind him in those early days. Dick Hern, the man who masterminded Brigadier Gerard's fabulous career and now trains for the Queen, is another racing success who owes a debt to Pope. For they were both fellow officers in the North Irish Horse. Says Michael: 'Towards the end of the war in Italy – over many, many grogs – we decided that when we returned to England I should set myself up as a trainer and he would be my assistant. We started with just two horses. He was a great help to me as my assistant for five years.

'In fact Dick and I helped organize the first Flat racing at Ravenna in Italy after the war. I believe that Dick rode the first winner there. There was a decent racecourse but it had huge bomb craters. We had to pinch a couple of bull-dozers and with the help of 200 prisoners we were able to flatten it out. Dick Ratcliff, for many years racing writer on the *Daily Mirror*, was also there at that time and trained some of the runners. We even organized a tote and made a good profit on the first two weeks. But then the Italians worked out some system of finding winning tickets and we caught one hell of a cold.'

Even now fun-loving Pope, a man with an excellent outlook on life, takes pride when he sees how brilliantly Eddery is galloping the racecourses of England – and indeed now the world. 'When I go to the races and he has a big winner I always give him a pat on the back and say: "Well done." And every single time he always comes back with the same answer: "Thanks . . . to you and Alvaro." '

And there are no prizes for guessing Pat's favourite restaurant in London. It is the little Italian restaurant in the King's Road called Alvaro.

6. 'Enfant Terrible'

The year of 1970 was an unforgettable one as far as Flat racing is concerned. The mighty Nijinsky became the first colt since Bahram to win the elusive Triple Crown and amassed £218 700 for his owner, the late Charles Engelhard, by winning his six races. That sum would have been boosted to well over £300 000 if Nijinsky had won the Arc de Triomphe but it is history – and still a constant talking point – that Lester Piggott was just pipped a head by Yves Saint-Martin on Sassafras.

For Pat Eddery, 1970 was the year for consolidating his position in the game. Thanks very largely to the amazing Alvaro – and Michael Pope's secret electrical trick – Eddery finished his second full season with twenty-three winners. Whenever trainers huddled together to discuss the up and coming stars the name 'Eddery' was always mentioned. But it was not only Pat's obvious talents in the saddle which were attracting attention. Often it was the way he had ridden out a finish, or gone for a manoeuvre in a race, which caused his name to be talked about. I can remember standing outside the weighing-room at Brighton one day that season talking to Chris Poole, racing writer of the *Evening Standard*, who combines two extreme hobbies in his life – listening to the haunting strains of music by his beloved Mozart and the ear-splitting roar of his equally much-loved Eastbourne Eagles speedway team. That morning we were chatting with Jimmy Lindley before racing when the young Eddery walked by carrying his riding gear in a carrier bag. 'Morning Jim,' said Pat with a typically friendly smile only to get the reply from the well-known senior jockey: 'Hallo – you reckless little bugger.' The greeting was in fact meant in good fun but there was no doubt in those early days of his career Eddery was seen as something of an *enfant terrible* by his colleagues. When Lester Piggott started he had exactly the same reputation. His father Keith Piggott told me once of a conversation he had with the late Ephie Smith just at the time when his son was making a name for himself. Referring to his fear nothing – or nobody – tactics Smith said: 'Keith, your lad is going to end up killing somebody.' Piggott Senior has always claimed that Lester was simply going for gaps which were his right and that there were too many old jockeys around at that time who should have packed up years before. That may have been the case and it has never really been disproved that Lester once turned to Gordon Richards, then way over fifty, in a race and shouted 'Move over Grand-dad.' In Lester's young days there were a few senior jockeys, very senior in fact, who could possibly have been genuinely afraid of the youngster breaking through the smallest of small openings. But in Eddery's case it was different. He was upsetting jockeys who were far from advanced in years. Looking back on this period of his life Pat is very honest:'Christ, I was never out of the Stewards' room. By then I was getting about one pound a week pocket money and my big love was going to the cinema. But the way I was going I was seeing two or three films every week – and I was always in the main role. I know what I was doing – I was simply trying too hard. I was desperately keen to ride winners and went for every little gap on the course. Then if I got into trouble I would try and push my way out of it. That made it all the worse. The other jockeys all thought that I was a bloody fool. At that time I would risk anything to be the first over the line. But I was riding horses who were not always very speedy and of course they were not able to get me out of trouble once I had got them into a difficult position. Still I learnt my lesson the hard way, forced to stay at home when all the others were off to the races.'

The season had started for Pat without any incident at Doncaster. Michael Pope had taken a four-year-old called Eskimo Boy to the south of France early in the year. Like that colourful Lambourn trainer Doug Marks, Pope realized that there was good prize money to be won and the races would give his horses a good warm-up for the Flat season in England. Ridden by a French jockey Eskimo Boy had finished second in the Prix Villeneuve-Bargemont at Cagnes-sur-Mer on February 8th but had run unplaced in the Prix D'Eze on the same delightful course on February 20th. Pope then entered him for the 1¾ mile Doncaster Spring Handicap worth over £1000 on the second day of the Flat season on March 24th. As Pat had ridden nine winners for Pope the previous season and looked a very mature young pilot the Streatley trainer had no hesitation in contacting Frenchie Nicholson to have the use of his ace apprentice again. Eskimo Boy, the only runner of the seventeen with the obvious advantage of a previous outing that year, seemed to have the race sewn up when Eddery switched him to the front three furlongs out and began to make his best way home. But George Kyle came with a late run on the Nigel Angus-trained Carry Off and pipped Pat by half a length. Kyle later transferred to Ryan Price's Sussex stables and seemed to have a good future in racing until tragedy struck in 1975 when he was killed in a car crash near Worthing. A passenger in the car, who suffered a leg injury, was Chris Leonard, who had been apprentice with Pat in the Nicholson days at Cheltenham.

Having been pipped by half a length in his very first race of the season Eddery soon showed that he meant business in the new campaign. He did not have a ride in the next race but promptly won the last race of the day, the French Gate Stakes on Lord Shrewsbury's Monaco Tan. This four-year-old had not raced as a two-year-old when he had been in training with Noel Murless. But he must have been quite highly thought of as a three-year-old initially as he ran in the Wood Ditton Stakes at Newmarket in April, 1969 when he finished eleventh ridden by Sandy Barclay. Ironically Eskimo Boy, who raced eight times that season for Arthur Budgett before joining Michael Pope at the end of the term, finished just three places in front of Monaco Tan, ridden by Ernie Johnson, who was then riding regularly for the Budgett camp and that same year had in his first ever ride in the Derby won on Blakeney. Pope was naturally delighted that he had won with his new purchase first time out but as the season wore on it became clear that Monaco Tan was no world-beater and in fact he never won again in seven outings that season; although Pat was third on him next time out in the Sandown Cup on April 24th and he was fourth on him in the Hampton Court Handicap at Ascot on May 2nd when he was backed down to 100–30 favourite.

He seemed to have a liking for being fourth because twice he filled that position later on at Newbury, once ridden again by Eddery and on the other occasion by Frankie Durr.

Pat got 'rave' reviews when he rode his second winner of the season. Riding for the very first time for Charlie Hall, the popular Tadcaster trainer, Eddery just got Humberside home by a head from Frankie Durr on Frontin in the Greasley Handicap over 1¾ miles. Humberside, backed from 30–1 to 100–8, led three furlongs from home but was headed inside the final furlong. But Eddery stuck to his guns and was well written-up for the way he rallied the six-year-old and inched ahead near the line. Warwick had slightly painful memories for Eddery after his fall there in July, 1968 but this in no way affected him when he easily won the Easter Handicap there on March 31st on Ballycano, who was trained by the then master of Manton, George Todd. Over the years no trainer made more skilful use of apprentices. Countless races were won by juniors whom Todd employed and most of them were instructed to use the same tactics – make every post a winning post and try to lead every inch of the journey. Ballycano was one such example and Eddery simply increased his lead coming into the final two furlongs while none of the other eight runners could get anywhere near him so that the winning margin was a comfortable four lengths.

Two years to the day after he had made his slightly nerve-wracking debut as a jockey on English soil Pat Eddery went back to Liverpool on Friday, April 3rd. But this time there were to be no instances of getting thrown off at the start. Riding Copper Witch in the Thursby Selling Plate Eddery again made all and won by five lengths. Copper Witch was trained by David Nicholson, who combined both riding over jumps and training jumpers and Flat horses from 1968 until he retired subsequently after a successful career in the saddle. Nicholson also gave Eddery the leg up for the next race on that Aintree programme, the Knowsley Stakes and this too proved a successful venture for Ally, who was owned by Beverley Brookes, older brother of Norton Brookes, the amateur jump jockey.

There was no real hint of the dramas that came later in the year for Eddery as he went about his daily work as an apprentice. By now he was well in the public eye and after his win on Philoctetes for Phil Bull the previous season, trainer Staff Ingham was one handler who was very keen to get hold of his services. His first ever win over the hallowed Newmarket turf came on April 30th when he won the Thurlow Handicap on Headley for Ingham. The first really big gambled winner of Eddery's highly promising career came at Kempton on May 8th when the George Todd-trained Francoise, making her debut for the season, was heavily backed from 5–1 down to 6–4 favourite for the Maypole Handicap. Here all of Pat's young enthusiasm and riding strength was needed to get Francoise home by a head from Mecca II. Peter Robinson, who first took out his licence to train in August, 1969 was another person who especially liked good apprentices on his horses. He was greatly impressed by the way Eddery, now only claiming five pounds, won the London Gold Cup at Ally Pally on June 9th, riding his three-year-old Angarrick. Later he absolutely hacked home by seven lengths in the William Hill Handicap at Ayr on June 20th – the youngster's first ever ride in Scotland. In between the two wins on Angarrick Eddery popped up at Kempton on June 10th with two rides for George Todd and won on them both. Bradfield won the Polymelus Handicap by three lengths from Lester Piggott's mount Marcus Brutus, and Welsh Windsor just got the better of Yellow River and Tommy Carter in the Silver Image Handicap by a short head. One of the newer trainers at this time was Simon Morant, who had established a small yard at Weathercock

House, Upper Lambourn. He had first taken out a licence in 1968 and he provided Eddery with the thirty-sixth winner of his career when Young Nick obliged in the Holloway Handicap at Ally Pally. Sadly the cash crisis in racing in the mid-seventies forced Morant to quit as a trainer but he retired with happy memories of his training feats with the good hurdlers Fintan Jay and Dan'l Widden.

Not forgetting the smart way Eddery had won the previous year's Vaux Gold Tankard on Philoctetes Staff Ingham was especially pleased when he lined-up Pat to re-unite with the then six-year-old in the £4542 Northumberland Plate at Newcastle on Saturday, June 27th. Having had two outings previously – he ran unplaced in the Great Metropolitan Handicap at Epsom on April 21st and the Chester Cup on May 6th when ridden by different jockeys – Philoctetes was allowed to start at 20–1. Sixteen runners lined-up for the start and when the field turned into the straight Eddery was placed thirteenth. But suddenly the son of Never Say Die lived up to his father's name and he came with a powerful late burst and got up by a length to hold off Maginot Line. Owner Phil Bull recalled: 'Actually I very seldom back any of my own horses and although I had backed Philoctetes when Eddery won on him the previous season I did not have a bet on him in the Northumberland Plate.' Eddery duly completed a double that afternoon when he won easily by five lengths on Rake Wood in the Wideopen Stakes. The winning trainer of Rake Wood was the legendary Arthur Stephenson, the brilliant Bishop Auckland handler better known for his remarkable feat of annually turning out over 100 winners over the sticks. Getting towards the end of June in the racing season and well on the way to his fiftieth winner Eddery had every reason to feel pleased with himself.

But Friday, June 26th at Chepstow on the previous day saw the first time Eddery had crossed swords with the stewards. And it must be said that from the way he was often seen barging through narrow gaps it was odds-on that it would not be the last time he would have to face the music. The day started frustratingly for Pat, who was fast emerging as a contender for the apprentices' crown but had an obvious rival in Ian Balding's good young apprentice Philip Waldron. In the first race of the afternoon, the Yale Maiden Plate for two-year-olds, Waldron on Silver Cedar just held on by a short-head to beat Eddery on Fools Desire. Eddery had one more unplaced ride before he received the leg up on Juicy Lucy in the Clifton Handicap over six furlongs. It was an incident which occurred two furlongs from home which spelt out disaster for Eddery and for the first time in his career resulted in serious trouble. The George Beeby-trained Dublin Decision was a warm favourite for the race and was in a prominent position two out until Eddery darted across to get to the rails on Juicy Lucy. Dublin Decision came crashing to the ground and David 'Flapper' Yates was indeed very fortunate not to receive serious injuries. Eddery and Juicy Lucy battled on and finished second behind Jolly Judge. Sadly there was no jolly judge about at Chepstow after racing that evening when the case of the fall of Dublin Decision was looked into. And the local stewards did not like what they had seen one little bit and after interviewing Eddery they informed him that in their opinion the fall of Dublin Decision was caused solely by him coming across to the rails too quickly. Eddery was suspended from riding for seven days and unlike several top jockeys, who have never been suspended in their lives, he became a marked rider at the tender age of eighteen.

Luckily for Pat the suspension did not start until the following Monday so he was able to ride at Newcastle the next day and did not miss the ride on Philoctetes in the Northumberland Plate, although it was the last day he was able to ride for a week. Looking back to his win on Philoctetes Pat says: 'I must admit that the win gave me a terrific thrill. I had been boxed in but managed to get out of trouble. I remember thinking about the Chepstow business and I was determined to go out with a winner and it was even better to win a big prize. When the Chepstow incident happened I knew I was in trouble. I just judged my crossing over a bit too finely and chopped the other fella off.' Pat was soon cursing his period of inactivity as the following Wednesday Yellow Flash won the Oxonian Stakes at Alexandra

Park with Geoff Lewis on board. Pat had already been booked for the ride and it was to be the first time he was to miss a winner due to suspension. Sadly for him it was not to be the last, but this was only a £665 event. There were bigger disappointments ahead.

Yellow Flash's trainer Michael Pope told me: 'I saw Pat after his suspension and naturally he was disappointed at missing a winning ride, particularly as he was getting involved in quite a battle for the apprentices' title with Philip Waldron. But he gave me a smile and congratulations after Yellow Flash had won. I was able to keep the youngster happy by offering him the ride the next time he ran.' Yellow Flash received a 10 lb penalty for his Ally Pally win in the Agricultural Handicap at Warwick on July 7th but Pat's five pound claim reduced the weight a little. Just two days back after his first suspension Eddery was back in the winners' enclosure for Yellow Flash won by two lengths from Nautical William. A day later Pat was again back amongst the winners, this time at Newmarket, when he won the Summer Handicap on Bradfield. This was his second win of the season on George Todd's useful stayer. Inca's Whistle continued his good run at Brighton that week and David Nicholson provided him with another winner when Bob obliged in the Aldersley Handicap at Wolverhampton on July 13th. At this stage of the season he was neck and neck for the apprentices' title with Waldron, although the good northern boy, Willie McCaskill was by no means out of it. Pat was having no weight trouble and his minimum weight was 7 st 4 lb, just three pounds heavier than he had been when he rode his first winner on Alvaro the previous season.

Pat made another successful raid on Scotland on July 21st for Peter Robinson. At this time during his career Pat was driven simply everywhere by either Frenchie or Diane Nicholson. The miles they must have clocked up putting the youngster onto the racing map must have been truly amazing. At Ayr Eddery won the Tennent Trophy Handicap on Brioche. This gave him the eighth win of his career in races valued at over £1000. Early in August he gained two more £1000-plus race wins when Brian Swift's Bold Strings

70

won the Brighton Challenge Cup and the Doug Smith-trained Christine won the New Victoria Cup at Nottingham. He also scored twice on Final Parade for David Nicholson early in August and won again on the reliable Bob. Things were really swinging for Eddery. The greatest moment of his still short but eventful career was just around the corner . . . and so too was his darkest hour.

When Pat was driven by Frenchie Nicholson to Haydock Park on Saturday, August 22nd he knew that he had seven rides on the seven-race card. None of his mounts were special. In fact as he gazed in the *Sporting Life* on the long motorway journey up from Cheltenham he realized that only one of his rides had actually been tipped by any of the daily newspaper tipsters. The one most papers picked out, Benoma, duly won the opening Old Boston Apprentices' Handicap at 5–4. Pat then went on to win the Wood Pit Auction Stakes on Durazzo for East Illsley trainer Gavin Hunter, who first took out a licence in 1966, having spent 2½ years as assistant to both Tom Jones and Atty Corbett at Newmarket. Punters and bookmakers could scarcely have realized what was about to happen when Mendi and jockey Peter Madden duly landed odds of 5–4 on in the Matthew Peacock Handicap with Eddery finishing third out of the four runners on Grisaille. But then the remarkable happened. Having won the first two races in brilliant style the ace apprentice then went on to win the next three races, thereby riding five winners in one day at the age of eighteen. Barry Hills' Floragold drifted from evens to 6–4 in the Wigan Sprint Handicap but Eddery, in unrivalled form, got up by a head to beat 11–8 favourite Misty Palm. There was an easy four lengths win for Clermiston in the Lyme Park Nursery Handicap and then Pat rounded off his unforgettable five-timer by winning on Vale Royale in the Hermitage Green Maiden Stakes for his guv'nor Frenchie Nicholson at 3–1. For any lucky punters who put Pat's five winners together in a speculative £1 accumulator there was a £1012 jackpot to pick up after the sixth race at Haydock that day. Eddery had one more ride that afternoon when he partnered Just Peggy in the West Lancashire Maiden Stakes. By now every betting shop in the country was buzzing with Eddery's success and there is a huge army of coincidence gamblers. That is how Just Peggy, running for the first time as a three-year-old and with no form whatsoever to recommend her chances, was trimmed in the odds from 33–1 to 7–1.

Just Peggy's odds were clipped dramatically at Haydock but lightning did not strike for the sixth time in the same place. Just Peggy was always in the back division and eventually finished sixth. The memory of riding five winners in a day at Haydock haunted Eddery for seasons and it was quite clearly in his mind on the rain-lashed day at the Lancashire course on the last day of the 1974 Flat season. For Lester Piggott, the ex-champion battling hard to regain his crown, could have pipped Eddery to the title if he had won on all his five booked rides that day. One kind hearted bookmaker actually had the nerve to quote Piggott at only 50–1 against riding the five-timer. I trust he did not attract any mugs. But Eddery did not rest until he knew that Piggott had failed to win on one of his rides, thereby making sure that he was the champion. As Pat said at Haydock on the eve of the finale: 'I rode five winners here once and none of them were all that much fancied. I am sure Lester will not give in until he knows that he cannot win the title.' The historians amongst the racing press were quick to delve into their records after Pat's five-timer. Lester Piggott has ridden five winners on one card but according to authentic records no apprentice has ever had five wins in one afternoon. By now everything in the Eddery garden was perfect. If any trainer or punter had not heard of Frenchie's latest riding prospect they certainly did after the Haydock bonanza. But as with the early days of Lester Piggott the impetuosity of youth was to darken an otherwise sparkling career.

When Eddery had suffered his ban earlier in the season following the inquiry into the Chepstow fall, the winning ride he had missed was Michael Pope's Yellow Flash. Now riding Yellow Flash in Brighton's Eric Simms Memorial Handicap on August 27th Eddery plunged head first into another heap of trouble. He started the day eight winners in front of Philip Waldron, thanks largely to the Haydock winner blitz. But it was a bad day all round for Pat because he rode in two later races that afternoon when Waldron won on favourites Primanda and Bodega to reduce the lead to six.

Brighton Stewards were quick to summon Eddery to their room after he had finished second on Yellow Flash, just two lengths behind the winner Grandrew. Eddery was found guilty of erratic riding and causing serious interference. The stewards heard the evidence from two experienced jockeys: Jimmy Lindley, who rode the winner Grandrew, and Edward Hide who rode sixth-placed Ouzo. Taking into account Pat's record the stewards handed out a second severe seven-day ban to begin on the next day. At the start of the 1970 season the Jockey Club had expressed their intention to tighten up on race-riding discipline among jockeys. Many jockeys were cautioned and suspended as the Jockey Club implemented their get-tough tactics, which were rightly introduced not only in the interests of the jockeys themselves but of the betting public. Eddery lost several good rides over the August Bank Holiday period and on the very day of the Yellow Flash incident not only did Waldron complete a double but the other challenger, Willie McCaskill, scored on El Credo at Carlisle. Commenting on Pat's second seven-day ban of the season Clive Graham, the late *Daily Express* racing correspondent, wrote at the time: 'A third infringement for Eddery would almost certainly lead to that ban which we poor motorists fear for similar peccadilloes.' Besides the Eddery ban, another interesting apprentice event took place at Brighton that day when seventeen-year-old Robert Edmondson rode his first winner, Optimistic Pirate proving an easy twelve lengths winner of the Waterhall Apprentices Handicap for Robert's master Paul Cole. Edmondson did not know what career to follow when he left school in his native York so he went along to the local employment exchange. The man in charge peered down at the minute Edmondson and said: 'For a chap your size I should think you could only be a jockey.' As luck would have it Paul Cole was circulating an advertisement for stable lads and a notice was actually on the wall of the York office when Edmondson walked in. One phone call, one interview with Cole and

Robert became an apprentice at Lambourn. Later in life he and Eddery became special friends, often staying away together for northern race meetings. When he started he only tipped the scales at 5 st 10 lb but he has shot up and a career as a jump jockey has looked a distinct possibility. Robert became champion apprentice in 1972 with forty-five winners. This, despite two seven-day bans, was the figure Eddery had reached by the end of August in 1970. In 1952 Joe Mercer had been champion apprentice with just twenty-six winners and David Yates only had to get twenty-four in 1963 to take the title. But 1970 and 1971 were freak years with Philip Waldron and Pat Eddery, both outstanding young horsemen, getting plenty of opportunities and riding the equivalent number of winners. In 1969 Clive Eccleston had clinched the championship with forty-one successes. Pat had passed that figure before he even started his second ban. The suspension did raise a few eyebrows. Like many Jockey Club rulings before and since the question of standardization was openly mentioned. For at the same Brighton meeting Bobby Elliott had appeared to commit a very similar offence. Yet while Eddery was stood down for seven days, Elliott got a three-day ban. Perhaps the stewards thought a stiff ban meted out to the young Irishman would curb his over-enthusiasm. Whether the two bans cost Eddery the apprentices' title we shall never know, but it is a fact that at the end of the season Philip Waldron had ridden fifty-nine winners while Eddery had to be content with the runner-up position with fifty-seven successes, although he did have a better average of 14.21 winners per 100 rides, compared to Waldron's 13.58. The best winning total by a champion apprentice since the war is Edward Hide's seventy-five in 1956, followed by Sandy Barclay's seventy-one in 1966 and the seventy-one gained by Pat Eddery a year after his narrow defeat by Waldron.

The year of 1970 was successful for Pat, although he would have loved just three more winners to pip Waldron for the apprentices' title.

Of his fifty-seven winners the trainers who gave him successful rides were: Pope (six), Ingham (three), Todd (seven), David Nicholson (six), Arthur Stephenson (four), Blagrave (three), Robinson (three), Doug Smith (two), Harvey Leader (two), Frenchie Nicholson (two), Ron Smyth (three), Dawson (two), and one apiece from Maxwell, Swift, Price, Charlie Hall, Ransom, Morant, Harwood, Murray, Hunter, Hills, Wragg, Barling, Gosling and Carr. Kempton seemed to be his favourite track that year with seven wins, the same as at Haydock, thanks to the five-in-one day. He scored five wins at Ayr and three each at Newmarket, Nottingham, Salisbury, Sandown, Windsor and Wolverhampton. After just two seasons of full-time race riding in the south only Chepstow, Lingfield and Yarmouth were courses where Eddery had yet to ride winners. Up to the end of the 1970 season he had won twenty-eight races from five to seven furlongs, eighteen between a mile and eleven furlongs, and twenty-one races at $1\frac{1}{2}$ miles and over. Only eight wins in his career at this stage had been gained on two-year-olds. At the close of Pat's third season he was well established and in answer to the seeming lack of two-year-old winners Frenchie Nicholson said at the time: 'Pat has had few opportunities to ride good two-year-olds as heavier jockeys usually get the pick until the Nursery season comes round. But I think few jockeys ride a young horse better. He has good hands and a steady head. He likes horses and has a natural understanding of them. He works well and tries hard and should continue to do well if he keeps on this way.' Headmaster seemed pleased with pupil Eddery judging by this end of term report. At Newmarket on October 3rd Eddery won the Wyck Hall Handicap on Jolisu for Tommy Gosling and lost his claiming allowance. As another ex-Nicholson pupil Cook observed: 'It is when you lose the allowance that the big test comes. Trainers have short memories and forget the good races you rode for them while you were claiming.' Eddery quit the racing scene at the end of 1970 as a fully fledged jockey. Now he was to ride against the Piggotts and Mercers with no weight advantage. It was indeed the big test but Eddery was more than capable of meeting it . . . despite the occasional flash of over-exuberance.

7. The Barling Connection

With his benign appearance and ever kindly outlook it was hardly surprising that Geoffrey Barling became known at headquarters as the 'Vicar of Newmarket'. It was a highly suitable name for a man who built up over the years the reputation of being one of the straightest figures in the game.

Barling retired at the end of the 1973 season but, like Pope, still has his record books which are so well dotted with the Eddery connection. Recalling how he first became involved with the Irishman Barling told me: 'It was mid-way through the 1970 season that I first spotted Eddery. He seemed a good young rider and I was keen to use him. His first ever ride for me came in the Royal Borough Handicap at Windsor on August 17th that year when he finished next to last on Legion. It was hardly a successful start but I liked the youngster a lot and gave him some more rides that season. Looking back through my records I see that he had five rides for me in all in 1970 and rode one winner.

'I had a gentleman's agreement with Frenchie Nicholson that I should, more or less, have first choice for Eddery. There was never anything written but we just had this understanding and it always worked out very well.'

The 1971 season saw Eddery's career move along in the expected manner. Having been pipped by Philip Waldron the previous year for the Apprentices' Championship, he made no mistake this time and his seventy-one winners clinched the title. Waldron had sixty-four. Pat's winners, which came from 655 rides, meant that he was ninth in the complete riders' list behind Piggott (162), Carson (145), Lewis (119), Murray (112), Mercer (89), Hide (84),

Starkey (80) and Durr (71). Only Carson and Murray rode in more races than Eddery – a clear indication of masterful organization on behalf of the youngster by his guv'nor Frenchie Nicholson. Anybody thinking that Eddery had never previously encountered a ding-dong battle for a title, when he was involved with Lester Piggott in 1974, could not have been more wrong. For the battle between Pat and Philip was a closely fought contest with neither side giving an inch. By the end of April, Eddery had gone four clear of his great rival and friend Waldron. But by the end of June it was Waldron who had a one winner lead. Pat regained the advantage at the end of July by a slender one win margin. By the end of August it was level pegging with fifty-two winners apiece. But by the end of September Pat opened up a 65–61 lead and it was on the basis of this that he finally won the title. His winning score of seventy-one equals Sandy Barclay's seventy-one of 1966 as the second highest total by a champion apprentice. Edward Hide had notched seventy-five in 1956 to win the title and his record still stands.

The year of 1972 was probably the most important in the transformation of Eddery from a much acclaimed Champion Apprentice to one of the really big names in racing. Not only did he join the small and élite band of high-class jockeys but he started to ride blue-blooded horseflesh worth thousands of pounds. Yet his initial experience in the wonder world of the Classics was almost identical to his debut race at the Curragh – he finished a long way last. In 1972 the link between Geoffrey Barling and Eddery was as strong as ever and the Newmarket trainer engaged Pat to partner the American-bred filly Golden Pawn in the 1,000 Guineas. Having her first outing of the season Golden Pawn was a 100–1 outsider and ran rather like it. Eddery sent her to the front from the word go and she led for over two furlongs but weakened and was quickly relegated to the last of the eighteen finishers.

If Eddery had been asked at this stage of his career which was his favourite horse he would have been hard pushed to answer. His love for the amazing Alvaro was still there but other horses were emerging to share his great affection. High

on the list was the four-year-old colt Erimo Hawk, a son of
Sea Hawk II. Geoffrey Barling takes up the story: 'The
British Bloodstock Agency contacted me and said that a
Japanese businessman called Schinichi Yamamoto wanted
to have some horses trained in England. This owner never
spoke English and never once came to this country to see his
horses run. It was rather an impersonal way to conduct
affairs but he certainly owned a nice horse in Erimo Hawk.'
In 1971 Eddery rode Erimo Hawk in his first race of the
season when he came home the winner of the twenty-eight
runner Humber Maiden Stakes at Ascot. Later that season
he also won the H. S. Persse Memorial Handicap at Kempton and the Final Stayers Stakes at Sandown. But it was as a
four-year-old that Erimo Hawk stole the headlines and Eddery
produced some fine riding displays on him.

'Again as a four-year-old Erimo Hawk won his first race
of the season, the Selfridge's Queen Prize at Kempton,'
recalls Barling. 'But it was when he won his next race, the
Paradise Stakes at Ascot in April, that I realized what a fine
horse he was. There were only three horses in the race and
he absolutely trotted up. I had him very fit at the start of
the season and he was one of those horses who really kept his
best form.' Rides in Classics, wanted by top-class trainers to
ride really good horses . . . everything was looking good for
Eddery. But yet again the one failing in his make-up was to
get him into hot water and put him on the sidelines. Looking
back on the incident in the Ladbroke Chester Cup on May
2nd Eddery readily admits: 'It was the worst thing I ever
did on a racecourse.' He cannot remember the exact details
of some of his other transgressions but this one is still clear
in his mind. Looking back he told me with a typical chuckle:
'I was riding a horse called Pirate Glen and pushed Lester
Piggott out on the final turn. I knew I was for the high jump
the moment it happened.' Lester was in fact on Ashleigh
while Eddery finished second, just a head behind Happy
Victorious. It came as no surprise to Eddery when he was
called into the Stewards' room. After the inquiry Pirate Glen
was disqualified and placed last and Ashleigh promoted to
second. Having found Eddery guilty of 'reckless' riding they

suspended him from May 4th for seven days. Yet again the stewards were not amused by Pat's seemingly wayward motto of 'win at all costs'. The film showed that he had not only pushed out Piggott on the last tight Chester turn but also squeezed his way through to finish second. Luckily for Eddery his ban did not start in time to rob him of the chance to ride Erimo Hawk in the Ladbroke Chester Cup the next day. Whether the suspension was on Pat's mind or not it is hard to say but he did not ride a good race on Erimo Hawk this time.

'The less said about that race the better,' admits Barling.

Further drama was to follow Erimo Hawk in his next race. This was the £18476 Ascot Gold Cup, the 2½ mile stayers race which is one of the many fascinating events in the Royal Ascot line-up. The previous year the Peter Walwyn-trained Rock Roi had roared home by four lengths. Later a test showed that an illegal trace of dope had been found and he was disqualified, the race being awarded to the Arthur Budgett-trained Random Shot. This time Pat Eddery on Erimo Hawk and Duncan Keith on Rock Roi were involved in a terrific battle up the Ascot straight with this valuable prize obviously between them. Rock Roi was almost unbackable at 11–4 on, but mighty cheers went up for him when he went ahead in the last few strides and finished first by a head. But it was obvious to even the most inexperienced racegoer that Rock Roi had hung badly in the final stages of the race and it was no surprise when the stewards immediately announced that they were holding an inquiry. Duncan Keith recalls: 'Rock Roi had previously been suffering from coughing and had a bit of a temperature. It was not the real Rock Roi who ran in that second Gold Cup. Halfway round I knew that he would not win. He was never giving me the usual super feel. I reckon that Erimo Hawk was always a little bit of a thief – not hundred-per-cent. In the final stages I produced a bit of a challenge to Erimo Hawk and sure enough he did not want to know, chucked it in and we got up in front again on the line. But I had rolled over on to him and had to lose the race. It was so annoying because of the business the previous year. If Rock Roi had been his proper self the second time he would have won the Gold Cup by ten lengths, on the bit, running away.' Says Erimo Hawk's trainer Geoffrey Barling: 'I was sure that he would beat Rock Roi if Pat Eddery rode the race I wanted him to. He simply had to wait until the final stages to make his challenge. I could see there had been some boring in the closing stages of the race and when they came back the first thing Pat said to me was "We will have to object". But I said that there was bound to be a stewards' inquiry and did not want to win the race on an objection – particularly as it was the Ascot Gold Cup. There was, of course, an inquiry and we were awarded the race.'

No objection was needed when Erimo Hawk and Eddery went on to win the Goodwood Cup Stakes on July 27th. He was backed down to 11–10 on and showed his class with an easy win over Parthian Plain and Hickleton. Franwin was the 100–1 outsider in the field of four that day and I recall John Banks, then in his heyday as a bookmaker and slaying his rivals daily in publicity gimmicks, offering a carrot to a holiday for two in Portugal for a fortnight. The flame-haired Scotsman handed out several carrots but was never in danger of having to foot the bill for any suntans. I might add that Franwin's trainer Albert Davison was none too happy about Banks' offer and when the horse did subsequently win a race later in his career the Caterham handler was quick to ask: 'Where is that bloody Banks now with his ruddy carrots?' Time had passed and while Davison was still training Banks had quit as a bookmaker. Recalls Davison: 'I only took Franwin there to tune him up for jumping and picked up £100 prize money for my trouble, so it wasn't a bad day's work.' After the Goodwood Cup Erimo Hawk was next seen in the Doncaster Cup on September 7th. They say that money talks in racing and it was certainly true that day as Erimo Hawk drifted from evens to 7–4 before finishing fourth of five. Lady Beaverbrook's Biskrah got up by a neck to hold off the French raider, Le Chouan, ridden by Yves Saint-Martin. After this Barling made the bold decision to give Erimo Hawk his final race of the season in the £100000

(Top left) Jimmy Eddery pictured while working as a stableman at Lewes in 1975 – a far cry from the height of his career in 1957 when he is seen *(top right)* after finishing second on Silken Glider in The Oaks. *(Below)* 17-year-old Pat wins his first ever race on Alvaro in the Spring Apprentice Handicap at Epsom, 1969.

The Royal Ascot sensation of 1974 which cost Eddery the ride on
English Prince in the Irish Derby. All three runners were disqualified –
Gloss and Eddery (right), Confusion and Starkey (nearest camera) and
Royal Prerogative (Goreham). *(Below)* The teenage Eddery and his
master, Frenchie Nicholson.

Eddery's first Classic win on Polygamy (far left) in the 1974 Oaks. Luckless Carson on Dibidale has lost his saddle. *(Below)* Pat Eddery, Peter Walwyn and Dr Carlo Vittadini are presented to the Queen Mother after Grundy's famous win in the King George VI & Queen Elizabeth Stakes at Ascot.

When champions clash . . . Piggott *(above right)* on Saritamer just gets
the better of Eddery on New Model in the 1974 July Cup at Newmarket.
But Eddery on Hard April *(below left)* wins the Sonning Court Stakes
by a head from Piggott on Peter Prompt at Sandown in 1974.

Prix de L'Arc de Triomphe at Longchamp on October 8th. This gave Eddery his first ever ride in Europe's richest race round the fabulous Longchamp course.

This was expected to be the Arc when Lester Piggott would finally break his duck. For fourteen years the maestro had ridden top class horses in the race but cruel luck had dogged his path. Nijinsky, Ribocco, Sir Ivor and Park Top were just four famous animals who did not win the huge autumn prize, which on their best form they clearly should have done. In 1972 the French-trained Hard to Beat was all the rage and almost to a man the gambling-mad Paris crowd were on the 6–4 'hot-shot'. But Lester could only finish a dismal eighth behind the filly San San, who equalled Mill Reef's record of the previous year of 2 minutes, 28 seconds. Fillies filled three of the first four placings and San San became the first female to win since 1953. Erimo Hawk was always in the rear and finally finished twelfth. Says Barling: 'We hoped for soft going but, as rarely happens in the Arc, it turned out to be quite firm. This was against Erimo Hawk but he still ran quite a decent race.' This subsequently proved to be Erimo Hawk's last ever race. Barling considers that he had developed a bad leg in the autumn and the run in the Arc on firm going probably did the final damage.

After the Pirate Glen incident at Chester earlier in 1972 Pat says: 'I was especially keen not to get in any trouble. I felt that I was maturing all the time and not going for the small holes that I would have gone for earlier in my career. I was riding better horses all the time and the winners were coming along nicely. I felt much more relaxed in myself.' But at Newbury on June 15th Eddery was back in trouble again and as the race was seen by racegoers it looked as though he could possibly be in for a much more serious penalty this time. The race was the Childrey Maiden Stakes for three-year-olds. In the race Pat rode Battle Hymn for trainer Jeremy Tree. Drama followed drama in the race. Brian Taylor sustained severe concussion when Water Colour came tumbling to the ground six furlongs from home and Geoff Baxter had to be rushed to hospital with a knee injury after his mount, Vraiment, fell as well. If that was not sensational enough for a Flat race, after Willie Carson, riding Beau of Serro, had beaten Geoff Lewis on The Admiral by a head, Lewis accused his fellow jockey of hitting his mount over the head. The stewards overruled Lewis's objection but on seeing the film found Eddery guilty of dangerous riding on Battle Hymn, who finally finished fifth. They considered that he had caused Baxter's fall on Vraiment. As is normal in cases such as this Eddery was officially reported to the stewards of the Jockey Club. With his record and all the dramas in the Newbury race the picture certainly looked black for Eddery as, accompanied by Frenchie Nicholson to whom he was still apprenticed, he visited Portman Square. But the stewards of the Jockey Club obviously saw the video tape of the race somewhat differently and Eddery was cleared of the charge of dangerous riding and he was able to plan his rides for Royal Ascot, which of course included the controversial one on Erimo Hawk.

The year of 1972 will always be remembered for the epic battle between Roberto and Rheingold for the Derby and all the intrigue that preceded it. Pat Eddery, at the age of only 20, finished third on Pentland Firth in his first ever Derby ride. This colt was also trained by Geoffrey Barling and Eddery rode him when in 1971 he made his debut in the Fulbourn Maiden Plate at Newmarket on July 6th. Pentland Firth finished sixth but there was plenty to like about this son of the Derby winner Crepello. Ironically another two-year-old went greenly down to the start that day for his first ever appearance on a racecourse – Coup De Feu, who finished second behind Broth of a Boy. Pat failed to take much notice of the runner-up having his first spin but he was to be associated with the horse in a remarkable way later on in his successful career. Says Barling: 'Pentland Firth and Eddery went on to win the Norfolk Stakes at Newmarket on July 31st and the Fitzroy House Stakes also at Newmarket on August 21st. He was shaping up into a really good horse.' When he gained his second win at Newmarket it was the then Jack Watts-trained Coup De Feu who was second, beaten by 2½ lengths. His next race was the Dewhurst Stakes at Newmarket on September 8th when he finished fourth behind Crowned Prince, who at that time was the most expensive yearling ever purchased, having cost a staggering £212000.

Pentland Firth's final race as a two-year-old was in the *Observer* Gold Cup on October 23rd when he finished a creditable third, beaten just threequarters of a length and two lengths by High Top and Steel Pulse. It is interesting to note that in this contest Rheingold was well beaten into eighth position. Pentland Firth was soon back into winning form in his first race as a three-year-old in 1972 and Pat Eddery was the rider when he took the Ladbroke Classic Trial at Sandown by a length and a neck from Charling and Rascolnik. Recalls Pat: 'Pentland Firth was a really good colt but whenever he ran we had trouble getting him into the stalls. I was always frightened that one day he would refuse point blank to go into them.' Lester Piggot partnered Pentland Firth when he finished second in the Predominate Stakes at Goodwood on May 17th. 'He should have won' is Barling's unhappy recollection of this race. Pentland Firth was backed down to 11–8 on but was pipped by half a length by Ron Hutchinson on Scottish Rifle. The dreaded moment finally came in the Ladbroke Derby Trial at Lingfield on May 13th when Pentland Firth, backed down to 7–4 favourite, simply refused to go anywhere near the stalls and despite all the handlers' attentions had to be withdrawn not having come under starter's orders. The race was subsequently won by Charling. Says Barling: 'He was a highly strung horse and this was why he sometimes acted this way. I had to get a certificate before he could run again.'

This was duly obtained and Pentland Firth's next race was the Epsom Derby on June 7th which saw Eddery riding in his first Derby – over the same course and distance where Alvaro had triumphed in April, 1969. Just three years from riding a first ever winner to taking part in the world's greatest Flat horserace was a fine achievement by Eddery. And those who stepped in and backed Pentland Firth at 50–1 certainly had a run for their money as the young Irishman was placed third behind Roberto and Rheingold, beaten only a short head and three lengths.

Pentland Firth did not quite emulate his father Crepello and win the Derby but it is worth noting that he was third behind a horse who went on to win the Benson & Hedges Gold Cup in a record time and a second who was never ever beaten in France and won the Arc de Triomphe at the end of his four-year-old career. Rheingold did not run in the Arc as a three-year-old. Lester Piggott rode him in the Benson & Hedges and was a sad fourth. It was a year later in 1973 that he switched rides with Yves Saint-Martin and finished a disastrous third at 6–4 on behind Moulton. But before the year was out Lester's Arc agony was all over and Rheingold came back to a hero's welcome at Longchamp. Pentland Firth was purchased by Barling from the Banstead Manor Stud at Cheveley, Newmarket, which produced Pasch (2,000 Guineas and Eclipse) and Pont l'Eveque (Derby). Says Barling: 'Pentland Firth was owned by Victor Hardy, who also had another horse with me – Tower Walk – so he was a lucky owner. Tower Walk won the Prix de L'Abbaye at Longchamp in 1969.' After the Derby Pentland Firth only had one more race in his career. Pat Eddery partnered him when he finished second behind Falkland in the Princess of Wales's Stakes at Newmarket on July 4th. Despite this defeat Barling was convinced that Pentland Firth would win the St Leger. 'During the year he had already beaten the blinkin' lot in the Leger and I thought he had a first-class chance,' says Geoffrey. Sadly, Pentland Firth met with an injury and was retired to stud in South Africa for a fee of £100000. Boucher won the St Leger for the all-conquering O'Brien-Piggott team. But if ever a race was run to suit one horse this was it and the snail-like early pace played right into Piggott's hands. Barling may have a point about Pentland Firth. At Epsom he beat Our Mirage by three lengths for third place but in the Leger Our Mirage was only pipped by half a length into second place by Boucher.

In 1972 Pat Eddery had seventy-four rides for Geoffrey Barling and thirteen winners. Says Geoffrey: 'While he was riding for me he was an absolute model of consistency. I never had any trouble with him and of course a lot of this was due to Frenchie Nicholson and his wife. They would never allow any funny business.

'Throughout my career I was always lucky with my young riders. Besides having the services of Pat Eddery on many occasions, Taffy Thomas was apprenticed to me at Newmarket. I had many other good boys but the best of them all was without doubt Ron Singer. He was a marvellous little kid. He was apprenticed to me and had ridden thirty-nine winners in his short career when he had a terrible fall at the Liverpool Spring Gold Cup in 1960 and suffered brain damage. He was unconscious for three months and had no chance of coming back into racing. I am sure that but for the fall he would be a household name today. I would love to know how he is getting on.' Purely by chance I was able to tell Barling of Singer's whereabouts. On a visit to the then Ladbroke headquarters in Ganton House, London, I was chatting to their much respected senior press officer Stanley Longstaff when a little fellow came into the office delivering a message. Said Stanley: 'That is an interesting chap. He is Ron Singer, who was top-class apprentice fifteen years ago.' Barling was interested to hear of Singer and to learn that Ladbrokes had kindly given him a special job as a messenger boy and general helper around their offices. Talking to Singer was remarkable for he is only now – fifteen years later – beginning to remember what happened in his fall. He told me: 'I joined Mr Barling as an apprentice straight from school in Bethnal Green. He was a good guv'nor and I was doing pretty well. We all lived in a hostel and got a dollar a week. Our clothes were paid for and we were all very happy. I just wish that I could be as happy again.' Singer admits that he has a bad memory because of the fall. He added: 'All my thirty-nine winners were in proper races against senior jockeys. I was an apprentice but none of my wins were in apprentice races. Soon after the 1960 season started I rode one winner and then partnered Cross-bill in the Liverpool Spring Cup at Aintree on the day before the Grand National. To this day I can't remember much about the race and the fall. I can just remember waking up in a strange hospital and asking "Where the hell am I?" I was told later that I had been unconscious for three months. I was involved in a fall and had been kicked in the head. Slowly things are coming back to me but I doubt whether I will be able to remember properly.' My formbook says that Cross-bill 'slipped up after yards'. The date was March 25th, 1960 and the race was won by Jimmy Lindley on High Perch, who was trained at Lewes by Towser Gosden. When I asked Singer if he remembered where he rode his first winner he was quick to answer: 'Yarmouth on a horse called Blue and Away. Not even a kick in the head could make me forget that occasion.' He still goes racing when he gets the opportunity. He talks with pride of fellow jockeys in his days – Harry Carr, Manny Mercer and Eph Smith. His story highlights the danger that exists in racing, not only over the jumps but also on the Flat. Liverpool has obviously claimed some victims in the Grand National. But many top riders have suffered terrible injuries there.

By the middle of August in 1972 another jockey, Duncan Keith, was losing his private battle with ill health. As first jockey to Peter Walwyn he had for some years been having trouble with his weight and attempts to beat the scales had only resulted in ill health. Way back in 1970 Keith had enjoyed a near miracle escape from a finish to his career. But let Duncan tell his story where it started for him, in the grim, poverty-stricken area of the Glasgow Gorbals. He says: 'I was apprenticed to H. E. Smyth at Epsom from 1953 to 1959. Then I had ten successful years with Walter Nightingall but after he died I decided to become a freelance. One day in the autumn of 1966 I was riding at Salisbury and Peter Walwyn, for whom I had ridden a few winners, came up and said: "What are you going to do next year? Would you like to ride for me?" Funnily enough the very same week Arthur Budgett contacted me and offered me a job as well and there was a little bit more money in his job. But I was so impressed with the way Peter Walwyn went about his job that I jumped at the chance. Even in those days when he only had about forty horses you could see that he was going right to the top of the training profession. He was so dedicated and trained and worked with his horses. That's

86

what really impressed me. He is not like some trainers who train their horses from bed and just shout the orders out of the bedroom window as the string move out early in the morning. Peter is a great guv'nor and I enjoyed every minute with him.' Keith did well for Walwyn but by 1970 there were already signs that Keith was having terrible weight problems. Finally he had to tell Walwyn: 'It's all over – my mind and body just can't take any more of this dieting.' Looking back to his first breakdown Duncan relates: 'I was having trouble with my thyroid glands and living on less than 800 calories a day. My metabolism was all wrong.' Finally Keith had to call a halt and visit a hospital. His constant fight to tip the scales at 8 st 6 lb finally sapped his strength and broke his heart. From a Dublin hospital bed he had to watch Lester Piggott stepping in for the chance ride on Humble Duty when she won the 1,000 Guineas. Says Keith: 'That was the only time that I did not ride the filly. Still, Lester did send me a case of wine when I came out of hospital.'

Six weeks to the day that Keith told Walwyn he was quitting he was back in the saddle and riding Long Till in the Epsom Derby. He had visited the Dublin specialist who also saved Barry Brogan's jumping career at one stage. Prior to this he showed what a miracle comeback it was by winning a £19 000 race in France. Long Till, who led the Derby field until five furlongs from home, finally finished eighth behind Nijinsky but Keith was back in business. He and Walwyn were a first-class team. Duncan was unlucky with Humble Duty and in fact the duo were very unlucky in 1969 when Duncan won £86 391 in prize-money while another £150 000 slipped from their grasp by a matter of inches. For in the Oaks, King George VI and Queen Elizabeth Stakes, Wills Mile and Imperial Stakes, Walwyn and Keith had to suffer the agony of close-up seconds.

By 1970 Duncan's daily diet was failing to stop excess weight. He told me: 'I was having a job to do 8 st 5 lb and felt terrible. I went to Folkestone on August 22nd and won on the favourite Cesarea in the Ivychurch Maiden Stakes. It was the last time I ever rode in public. Two days later I set off to Brighton not knowing that I would never ride a race again. The thyroid glands were upsetting me like hell and I had no salt left in me. God knows how I even drove to Brighton. My hands just seized up on me. My body couldn't operate as my mind wanted it to. When I finally got to Brighton I felt like death and I was due to ride two very much fancied rides in the first two races. I simply decided there and then that I was retiring. If I had kept going I would have killed myself. There's no shadow of doubt about that. I sat down in the weighing-room looking as white as a sheet and Frank Morby replaced me in the first race and won on Floridor for Peter Walwyn. It was the very end for me.'

The thirty-four-year-old Scotsman certainly made the right decision. He had ridden twenty-four winners that season but there was little doubt that he was driving his body very near to the point of no return. Besides his ill luck with Humble Duty he also finished first past the post on Rock Roi in the Ascot Gold Cup in successive years only to lose the race twice. But he does have happy memories of riding such good animals as Humble Duty, Lucyrowe, High Hat, I Say, Rock Roi and his 1965 2,000 Guineas winner Niksar. His career began in 1954 and his first winner was on Zator at Folkestone – ironically the last course he ever rode in the silks. For Walwyn he had 183 winners and but for his grim battle against the scales who knows what could have happened. He was only thirty-four when he quit, relatively young for a top-class jockey. Racing is full of fascinating instances of what might have happened. If Keith had been more impressed with the thought of joining Arthur Budgett's stable instead of Peter Walwyn he might have won two Derbys on Blakeney and Morston. We shall never know, of course, but it is an interesting thought. Keith had a good long rest when he finally quit but was always keen to set himself up as a trainer. Finding suitable stables was quite a problem but Keith finally set up at The Red House, Littleton, Winchester, Hampshire. I am delighted to say that he is making a success of training with a small string and this dapper little character can usually be seen at the races or as an interested buyer at the sales. Not surprisingly his face looks a great deal chubbier these days and he looks far more relaxed now that he does not have to think about every single morsel which passes his lips. He is now a much happier character and tips the scales at 10 st 2 lbs. Mid-way through the 1975 season he told me in his broad Scottish accent, which has not diminished despite all his years in the south: 'I ride out every morning and I reckon I am riding better than ever. I hope to train a few horses over the jumps and, who knows, you may one day see me riding a couple of hurdlers.' As I have mentioned, Keith has made the successful switch from jockey to trainer and has a good band of owners behind him. Hillandale was his first ever winner – ironically also at Folkestone – and it was also ironical that Keith should saddle this colt to win the 2,000 Guineas Trial at Kempton in the spring of 1975 for he also won this race as a jockey on Niksar before going on to take the 2,000 Guineas proper at Newmarket. Says Duncan: 'I also won the Kempton Trial on Penny Stall, who was the first winner ever owned by Lord Marks. He called it Penny Stall as that was how he started before going on to have the huge Marks and Spencer chain of stores.'

Duncan also recalls happily winning on Vienna in France, which was Sir Winston Churchill's first winner there. 'You'd have thought we had won ten Derbys to hear the reception. It was fantastic,' he recalls. He thought he had the 1971 Derby well sewn up on Linden Tree until the great little Mill Reef loomed onto the scene. To this day he thinks he should have won the 1969 1,000 Guineas on Lucyrowe, who was trained by Peter Walwyn. 'She was a very hard puller,' he says, 'and to make the matters worse as I tried to restrain her I was bumped and bored all over the place. I never had her really balanced and we could do no better than finish fifth. But we beat the winner, Full Dress II, at Ascot.' Duncan also has many other claims to fame but none perhaps as rare as jumping the famous Pond fence at Sandown just before a Flat race. One of Bill Wightman's horses, Runnymede, took off with him on the way to the start. He bolted through an opening onto the adjoining jump course and went full pelt for the Pond fence. Runnymede and Keith negotiated the fence together but to this day Duncan admits: 'I did not have much to do with it. My experience in the show-jumping ring may have helped a little.'

Peter Walwyn speaks very highly of the Keith association. In the early days he helped to put the Seven Barrows stable more and more into the big prize-money. But when the little Scotsman was forced to quit in mid-season Peter had to make a snap decision. Looking back Peter recalls: 'Pat Eddery had ridden for me a few times and I was impressed. I had heard unofficially that he was on the stewards' black list because of one or two incidents. But I was keen to get him.' Geoff Baxter, another young up and coming rider at this time, was another choice mentioned to replace Keith. He had been apprenticed to Arthur Budgett and was a fine horseman, having won the valuable Prix Foy on his first ever ride in France. But one telephone call from Walwyn to Frenchie Nicholson secured the services of Pat Eddery and a brilliant championship-winning team was moulded together.

8. The Master of Seven Barrows

Drive along one of the country lanes just outside Lambourn, the horse-mad village set in picturesque Berkshire downland, and you could be forgiven for failing to spot the signpost which simply reads 'Seven Barrows $1\frac{1}{2}$ miles'. Seven Barrows received its name because it was an isolated spot and ancient Britons constructed about twenty huge burial barrows. There was an ancient settlement on the highest point of the downs and communal graves were situated there. In all there were about twenty graves but the spot received its name because in one place there were seven barrows extremely close together. In ancient times this was a deserted and rather deadly area. But today there is nothing deadly about the place. All is alive and well with an equine empire of 100 horses treading the lush carpet of the country's most perfect gallops. Seven Barrows is now the training establishment of a champion – Peter Walwyn. A man who has shattered all training records and forged a great partnership with his stable jockey Pat Eddery. The success story of Eddery in recent years has linked closely with Walwyn, a remarkably gifted man who has turned Seven Barrows into a winners' factory. Once Seven Barrows was a burial spot. Now it is something of a graveyard for bookmakers as they see over and over again the all-conquering Walwyn-Eddery double act stealing the show.

See the action in the tiny Lambourn village square around seven o'clock each morning and it soon becomes clear that this is the town of horses. Stable lads, complete with jodhpurs and tweed caps, dash in all directions on their way to work. Most of them visit the local newsagent to pick up their copy of the *Sporting Life*. It is a fairly typical village setting with the church gazing down on the local hostelry. The lych-gate of the village church gives the first insight into the Seven Barrows story. For it was erected as a memorial to Charles Jousiffe, the man who first put Seven Barrows on the racing map. Jousiffe was a big, roly-poly farmer who took a keen interest in racing. Like many people of his size he was a jolly character, keen to slap his friends heartily on the back and forever joking. Two Derby winners have been trained at Seven Barrows – one, of course, was the Pat Eddery-ridden Grundy in 1975 and the other one a very interesting horse called Kettledrum, who won the Derby in 1861. Kettledrum was probably exercised on the same area of the gallops where Grundy was to work over a century later. Kettledrum was bred in the Burnley area of what is now industrial Lancashire. He was owned and bred by Colonel Townley, a member of a well-known Lancashire Catholic family. History relates that Kettledrum was actually rather a lucky Derby winner as the red-hot favourite Dundee, who had immaculate form, broke down in the straight. Kettledrum was trained by a man called Prince prior to Jousiffe's arrival at Seven Barrows. Jousiffe was an extremely talented trainer and the best known of his Seven Barrows successes came with Bendigo, who carved out a name in racing history as one of the greatest weight-carriers of all time. Bendigo never ran as a two-year-old and in fact made his debut as a three-year-old in the autumn of 1883 when he was unplaced in the Cesarewitch. Remarkable as it now seems, Bendigo's next race was the Cambridgeshire, just two weeks later, in which he triumphed. In 1886 Bendigo left Seven Barrows to become the first horse to win the initial running of the Eclipse Stakes. Eighty-eight years later another Lambourn horse won the Eclipse, when Eddery steered home the shock winner Coup de Feu. Jousiffe trained with great success and Bendigo pulled off another first in the initial running of the Jubilee Handicap at Kempton, to celebrate Queen Victoria's Jubilee year in 1887, when he again triumphed. Bendigo was owned by Major 'Buck' Barclay, who had first bred him as a potential point-to-pointer.

When Surefoot won the 2,000 Guineas in 1890 Jousiffe was convinced that he had another Derby winner at Seven Barrows. Such was his confidence that he backed the colt to win a fortune. But, alas, Surefoot did not follow in Kettledrum's footsteps. It is a widely held theory that when Jousiffe died prematurely of a heart attack soon after the Derby it was the excitement of a possible Guineas-Derby double which had contributed to his downfall. But it must also be said that he was a man of immense size, over twenty-two stone, and was in the category of people always likely to suffer from a heart attack. Soon after his death the lychgate at Lambourn church was erected in memory of the first well-known master of Seven Barrows. On his death the house and stables were taken over by Joe Hartigan's uncle, Garret Moore, who had already, as a gentleman rider, won the 1879 Grand National on his own horse Liberator.

Next trainer to keep Seven Barrows on the winning map was Harry Cottrill, father of the former Newmarket trainer and colourful personality Humphrey Cottrill, who retired at the end of the 1974 Flat season. Harry Cottrill had previously trained at Foxhill shortly after the First World War. Among his patrons was the legendary Jimmy White – one of the biggest gamblers racing has ever known. Starting out as a humble builder's labourer in Rochdale, White amassed a huge fortune by various methods on the Stock Exchange. He was also extremely clever at landing coups on the Turf. But sadly he became so depressed at one period when his shares were doing badly that he sent all his staff away to Swindon and then poisoned himself. The irony of the situation was that if White had waited just a few more days he would have become a millionaire all over again. All his shares, which had plummeted to rock bottom, suddenly shot back up again. But by this time White had committed suicide. Cottrill moved to Seven Barrows after the stables and house had been empty for quite some time. Of the many winners Cottrill sent out from Seven Barrows three were outstanding. Irish Elegant became a brilliant, weight-carrying sprinter. Adam's Apple won the 2,000 Guineas in

1927 before being beaten by Call Boy in the Derby, while Lovely Rosa won the Oaks in 1936. Recalling the days of his father at Seven Barrows, Humphrey Cottrill told me: 'It was a very isolated place, ideal for training horses. But the stable lads had to walk three miles out from Lambourn every morning and then back again in the evening. The lads got fifty bob a week and were pleased to do the job. The famous Seven Barrows were, and still are, big humps in the ground. Perhaps the clearest memory I have of Seven Barrows is the big fire there in 1937 which destroyed all the stables. The ones there today were all built since. Seven or eight horses were killed in this terrible fire. We never discovered how it all started but it made a real blaze and a half. One theory was that a rat had nibbled through a fuse and created a spark. There were all kinds of theories but that was the most popular. For two or three days horses were running wild all over the Downs and it was a hell of a job getting them all back again and restabling them.' After Cottrill Senior left Seven Barrows the stables came under the control of the Craven estate.

In 1956 Peter Walwyn held the licence for his cousin Helen Johnson Houghton at Blewbury. Even from an early age Peter was interested in horses and, of course, his cousin Fulke Walwyn had started out on his fabulous career as a National Hunt trainer after an equally successful one as a jump jockey. Peter was refused a commission in the Royal Scots Greys on medical grounds but during National Service he did become a full corporal in the Intelligence Corps. Later Peter, whose father Colonel Taffy Walwyn was a great horseman, had his first taste of a racehorse stable when he joined Geoffrey Brooke at Newmarket for four years. It was after this spell at headquarters that Peter took over the licence at Blewbury. He trebled the size of the string but in 1960 bought Windsor House at Lambourn and set up on his own, although there was no sign of a horse in his yard. Here again a coincidence shaped the future of things to come.

From 1914 to 1919 a young soldier in the 12th Lancers was fighting the Germans in Gallipoli, France and Belgium. His name was Percival Williams and ironically another soldier in the next troop was Geoffrey Freer. Recalling how events brought Walwyn his first horse, Williams told me at his Hereford home: 'Geoffrey Freer was a fellow cavalry officer in the Lancers – he was in the next troop. Towards the end of the war when we were chasing the Germans just outside Mons five of us officers were hit by H-E shells. Two were killed outright, two of us were unconscious and miraculously the last one was all right. I was more than half disabled and was invalided out. Years later I had the odd horse or two in training with Humphrey Cottrill at Newmarket. When I became a little older I wanted the horses to be trained nearer my home so that I could go and see them. I was advised to go to Lambourn as that was much nearer. I asked several people who would be the best trainer to go to. Both the senior vet at Newmarket and Geoffrey Freer, who was then a handicapper and head of Newbury racecourse, told of a young man who was just starting out on his own. Of course, both the vet and Freer told me never to tell Peter Walwyn how he had been recommended to me as they were still very much involved in racing. I happened to be up at Newmarket and asked Colonel Dick Poole to introduce me to Walwyn. Actually I was master of the Four Burrow Foxhounds in Cornwall from 1922 to 1965 when my son took over from me. I reckoned at eighty it was time to pack up jumping over the stone walls of Cornwall. I was really more interested in fox-hunting than horseracing.

'I still have the two mares who have produced my horses. Aunt May was twenty years old in 1975 and it cost £100 for the mating with Roc du Diable which produced the colt Be Hopeful, which was the first horse Peter Walwyn had in his yard at Windsor House, Lambourn. Be Hopeful was a wonderful servant and in his career won twenty-seven of his 117 Flat races and was placed forty-two times. My other old mare is Ma Marie, who was nineteen years old in 1975. She is the dam of Pasty.' When I inquired from Percival Williams how the daughter of the Raffingora–Ma Marie mating came to get this name he told me: 'For years and years, with my interest in fox-hunting, I have shown hounds at the Peterborough Hound Show. I once had a bitch who came from Cornwall so I called her Pasty. She became champion bitch at the Peterborough show so when the filly came along I named her after the dog. My other good mare Mabel was the dam of May Hill.

'Be Hopeful was Peter's first horse and he did us wonderfully well until he broke a leg as a fourteen-year-old veteran. Actually I sent Peter another horse called Love Day, who was by Abernant but she was useless – not worth a mention.' Be Hopeful became one of the fascinating parts of Derby week. He was part of the scene along with the top hats, fairgrounds, lords, ladies and gypsies. He ran at eleven successive Derby meetings, winning twice and being placed four times. Said Peter Walwyn: 'I could not have asked for a more wonderful horse to start with. He was always a huge favourite in the yard. He was a bit weak and backward as a two-year-old and that's why I only ran him once. But since then he was never sick and his legs were like bars of iron. He knew so much about training he almost trained himself.' Walwyn started with Flat horses and jumpers. His first ever winner was Don Verde, who won a novice-hurdle at Worcester on November 22nd, 1960. He was ridden that day by John Lawrence, now Lord Oaksey. Recalling those times the likable television personality and gifted writer told me: 'I remember Don Verde was a very nice horse. He was a half-brother to Zanzibar but sadly he was killed later that season when he fell in the County Hurdle at the big Cheltenham Festival Meeting. We were at the last and he just fell, landed on his head and broke his neck. Another horse I rode for Peter in those days was Royal Spirit, who I think he bought at Newmarket for his wife. We arranged to have a really good bet on him second time out at Ludlow, but as so often happens, he fell at the second hurdle. Still he trotted up at Worcester and won again at Leicester.' Walwyn's first ever Flat win came when Snaefell won at Worcester, ironically the scene of his first jump winner.

It was a chance friendship between Percival Williams and brother officer Geoffrey Freer which led to the recommendation of Peter Walwyn getting his first ever horse, Be Hopeful. And it was a chance conversation which led to Peter taking over Seven Barrows.

Derrick Candy, who trained just one mile away from Seven Barrows, explains: 'In 1960 I had bought Seven Barrows from the Craven Estate, who at that time owned most of the land in that area. I had never lived there as I always operated from the Kingstone Warren. But when I bought Kingstone Warren I had to have Seven Barrows as well as they both came under one lot. I simply inherited David Hastings as a tenant. It is completely true that the sale of Seven Barrows to Peter took place because of a casual conversation between my wife and him. I think that our two strings of horses happened to meet down one of the many lanes and my wife asked him whether he would consider buying the yard. I sold him the house, the yard and 300 acres, which included the famous Farringdon Road gallops. I kept three other gallops and my son Henry has used them since my retirement. Peter Walwyn has been a great success. It is marvellous as he is such a good chap.'

Walwyn readily admits that he had to scrape together all his finances to make the big move to Seven Barrows. But the gamble paid off and from a small string of thirty-five horses and as many boxes he now boasts the most talent-packed yard in England and Ireland with 100 boxes. His gallops are the envy of all other trainers. In the mid-summer of 1975 when there was a spell of several weeks without rain the gallops at all the training centres became rock-hard. John Sutcliffe at Epsom summed up the frustration there when he said: 'You couldn't work a horse flat out on the gallops. It's as hard as a road. Peter Walwyn and Barry Hills are winning all the races because they are the ones who can get their horses fit on their gallops.' Barry Hills, near neighbour of Walwyn at South Bank, Lambourn also uses Peter's gallops. It is the $1\frac{1}{4}$ mile sawdust gallop which is so important and sneaks an obvious advantage over other trainers. He also has a covered indoor ride where his string usually start their morning work-out.

Shortly before Grundy ran in the King George VI and Queen Elizabeth Diamond Stakes I visited Seven Barrows and saw the morning gallop. If ever there was a case of watching a master going about his job, this was it. An early morning sunlight sneaked through the trees of Seven Barrows as his lads arrived in their cars. The success of the yard and its financial rewards are reflected in the mode of the lads' transport. There is not a bicycle in sight. Bang on the dot of 7.30 a.m. the tall, lean figure of Walwyn emerges from his house. In long, narrow jodhpurs he looks even taller than the figure we see on racecourses, usually with binoculars in one hand and a much-fingered formbook under his other arm. 'Come on, you jockeys, let's be having you,' shouts the stableman and within seconds out of every box strides a magnificently groomed animal, fully prepared for his day's exercise. On this occasion all thoughts were on Grundy and his forthcoming race at Ascot. Walwyn got the leg up on the six-year-old Spring Stone saying: 'Lovely horse. Won a hurdle race last season, you know.' One sensed the electric atmosphere in the yard when Matt McCormick emerged with Grundy, already sold to the National Stud for £1 million. Walwyn is clearly on edge at times like this. He lives every minute for racing and his horses. Total involvement is his secret. He trots into the centre of the covered gallop while the rest of his first lot of three-year-olds gradually works up a good pace in the outer circle. Every horse is scrutinized like a priceless jewel. After a period in the covered gallops Walwyn heads the string up onto the gallops. Leading about thirty-five horses in a line he could be mistaken for a Hollywood cavalry officer leading his men. But this is no fairytale. On reaching the gallops they split up into different groups for their brisk workout. Walwyn sits proudly on Spring Stone as he watches the main horses cross the narrow road on their return trip to the stables. 'Patch, Grundy – doesn't he look well? May Hill, One Over Parr – I really only got her right for Haydock. A Royal Palace colt, a Derring Do, a Roan Rocket filly . . .' So it goes on and you can sense the immense pride in the man as he watches his horses. Back in the yard it is a quick question time. 'Go all right, Bill? He went well, didn't he, Peter?' Every stable lad reports back on how the gallop has gone. There is no mistaking the loyalty towards Peter from his staff. As the buckets and brooms come out after the first lot the telephone line to Seven Barrows is already buzzing. The current day's runners are already being dispatched into the waiting box. Everywhere there is action.

One man who has played a big part in the Walwyn success is his head lad Ray Laing, who was with him when he first started. He is the man who supervises the feeding of Walwyn's wonder string. Yet if he walked onto a racecourse probably only a handful of people would know him, for he is strictly the backroom boy. The man who makes sure the horses are fed properly and kept physically sound for Walwyn to turn his genius to the job of training and placing horses. In thirty-eight years in racing Ray has never seen a Derby. He watched on television from his top-storey council flat when Grundy triumphed at Epsom. His job is not amongst the afternoon excitement of a racecourse but at the crack of dawn each morning at Seven Barrows. In his riding career he had one winner for Basil Jarvis at Newmarket. Now he has a staff of forty under him and is a vital cog in the Walwyn winners' factory. Relaxing in front of the television Ray has had many wonderful moments to enjoy. But at 5.30 each morning his alarm clock rings away and it is back to work to feed yesterday's heroes. Walwyn's assistant-trainer is Jeremy Speid-Soote, who was previously a trainer in his own right. Before that he was a jump jockey with Ryan Price and probably never quite reached the heights that his talents deserve.

Equally important in the Walwyn success story is his wife Virginia, better known as 'Bonk', who usually rides out with one lot, often two. She drives Peter to the races and has played a very vital part in the transformation of a man who once trained in a small yard before becoming England's champion trainer having sent out 700 winners in only ten years at Seven Barrows. Percival Williams told me: 'Peter's wife does not receive half the mentions she should. She is also very hard working. Peter, of course, is a wonderful trainer.

99

I only have two horses with him but he studies them as well as he would for somebody who has a string of horses. He looks after the small owner so well. I am sure it is his hard work that is the secret. His wife's father was master of the West Kent Foxhounds for years so I have a tie with him. Pat Eddery has done wonderfully well but he had a fine tutor in Frenchie Nicholson. For one so young Pat is so shrewd.'

When Eddery was voted Jockey of the Year by the Horserace Writers' Association in 1974 it was my pleasant task to write a short article on him for the annual brochure. Peter Walwyn's praise was predictable – but very true. 'He is a lovely jockey. He has a beautiful balance. He is very uncomplicated and never worries about money – just wants to ride winners. I spend hours on the telephone to him, just chatting away about horses. I will always back him to the hilt. Never once have I heard criticism of him from one of my owners.' Pat's praise of Walwyn is equally sincere. He says: 'He is the greatest guv'nor in the world. There can't be a better one. He never confuses me with a lot of orders. He just lets me get on the horses and often allows me to ride my own kind of race. He never ties me down with too many orders. He gives you so much confidence that you go out for a race really wanting to do your very best for him.'

Walwyn admits that he can flare up at times. But if there was ever a case of the bark being worse than the bite this is it. He has total involvement with the horses and with such a vast string it cannot be roses all the way. Many a pressman has had a short, sharp ear-bashing for something he has written about one of his horses. Others have also felt the whiplash of his tongue when seeking information after one of his more fancied runners has been beaten. But taken overall this is to be expected. If you build up your thoughts to believe you have a world-beater in your yard, which subsequently runs a 'stinker', you hardly want a pressman immediately asking, 'Where can you possibly run him now after that?' When Grundy was beaten at York I suspect Walwyn would willingly have gone straight home. But even though his dual Derby winner was well beaten into fourth place he was still big enough to face the press with their searching questions. I can think of a lot of owners and trainers who would have been less honest and forthright. One incident in August of 1974 highlighted Walwyn's honesty. I telephoned him to check some running plans but he told me: 'I have closed down.' He went on to explain that his horses had been hit by an outbreak of the virus and he would not be having any runners until the illness was cleared up. He said: 'I am not running my horses for the benefit of the bookmakers. I have got to think about the public as well as my owners.' So instead of semi-fit horses running up and down the country, bound to have been backed for thousands of pounds, Walwyn had a break and this was only one example of his forthrightness.

In 1971 he had to suffer the horror of losing the Ascot Gold Cup with his brilliant stayer Rock Roi when it was found that two grammes of a drug called Equipalazone had been administered. Not only did the owner, Colonel Roger Hue-Williams lose the £12429 prize-money but Walwyn was fined £100. But the stewards of the Jockey Club completely exonerated both Walwyn and head lad Ray Laing of all blame and they were acquitted of any corrupt practice or intent. Rock Roi was unlucky in two respects. For he beat Random Shot, the promoted Ascot Gold Cup winner, twice as easily at Goodwood. And even if the treatment had worked any therapeutic effect, it would have worn off long before the Gold Cup. The actual dose was given four days and ten hours before the race so it could hardly have affected the horse's performance. Still, the Hue-Williams family stuck by Walwyn and it was doubly cruel that a year later Erimo Hawk should be awarded the race on a disqualification. Walwyn told me: 'It was the most ghastly experience to win a race like that and then lose it. I never want to go through that torture again. It was terrible. To say I was keen to win the race a year later was the understatement of the century.' Those were unhappy days for Walwyn but he has had many a sunny one since. There was, however, another example of how luck can turn cruelly in racing when Peter's Linden Tree ran in the 1971 Irish Sweeps Derby. Linden Tree had been second behind Mill Reef in the Epsom Derby and with Paul Mellon's great little super star out of the way he seemed to have the Curragh race at his mercy. His only rival appeared to be Irish Ball but he had already shown him the way home at Epsom. There was drama galore when the starting stalls opened as sixteen of the runners came speeding out of the gate but not Linden Tree. He bucked, swerved and finally trailed in lengths behind the rest of the field. Said Peter Walwyn: 'His tail might have been caught in the back gate of the starting stall.' It was a truly remarkable and unlucky business. Especially as the winner of the race was Irish Ball who had finished two lengths behind Linden Tree at Epsom in the Derby.

Statistics can often be misleading but when it comes to hard cash earned in racing and the races won they clearly show how successful some stables have been. Walwyn's bonanza has simply rocketed along. In 1971 he won £62 680 in prize-money with sixty-one wins from thirty-six horses. In 1972 it was £60 519 with fifty-five wins from thirty-three horses. In 1973 it was £124 601 with eighty-seven wins from forty-nine horses. In 1974, when incidentally he was only forty-one years old and had only been training for thirteen seasons, he won a record-breaking £206 445 with ninety-six wins from fifty-four horses. These figures only include wins in England and in 1974 he topped the magical 'ton' with the aid of wins in Ireland and France. A year later there was no doubt about his century for when Pat Eddery won the Sancton Maiden at York on September 3rd on Ormeley this was the 100th winner trained on English soil by Walwyn in 1975. Ormeley reached the Walwyn century in style as he clipped .60 seconds off the electrically-timed course record for two-year-olds over one mile with a time of 1 minute, 40.80 seconds. Discussions have always gone on about who actually holds the record for the number of winners trained in England in a season. Bill Elsey's grandfather, William Elsey, trained 124 winners in 1905. But it is not totally clear how many of the winners were actually under rules. Other figures, some even higher than 124, are mentioned before the turn of the century but again it is impossible to state whether they were official races as we now know them. Before the Great War several trainers are reported to have turned out over 100 winners a year but I think Walwyn has the target of 124 to beat to clinch the title outright as the man to train most winners in England in a full season under Jockey Club rules.

Walwyn's greatest triumphs have been the Classic wins with Humble Duty, Polygamy and Grundy but he takes almost the same satisfaction from winning a small maiden race at Warwick or Bath. When his brother-in-law Nick Gaselee won an amateur race for him on Great Guns at Goodwood in 1974 there was natural excitement. 'Will he run again?' enquired a pressman. 'Yes, of course,' said a beaming Walwyn. 'Why not? He has taken nothing out of himself . . . and anyway I just love training winners.'

Already Peter has the immense satisfaction of seeing grandchildren of his first horses now in training in his yard. He admits: 'I just love being with my horses. Often you train by instinct and the more time you spend with them the better.' Once in a television interview Walwyn took a friendly swipe at some of less athletic rival trainers when saying: 'You can't train horses by sitting in a car watching them go by.' He readily admits: 'If I could not train horses I would be unemployable. There is nothing else I want to do but train winners.'

Walwyn and Eddery have two things in common. All they want to do is to train and ride winners. And they have immense loyalty to each other. They are the perfect blend of trainer-jockey. When Pat Eddery was suspended and missed the winning ride on English Prince in the Irish Derby, Yves Saint-Martin stepped in. The Hue-Williams family were keen that the French ace or Lester Piggott should ride the outstanding English three-year-old colt of 1974 in the Great Voltiguer Stakes at York. But Peter Walwyn stressed that if 'P. Eddery' – as he often calls him – did not have the ride the horse would have to leave the yard. Says Walwyn: 'I will always back him to the hilt.'

They are the ideal combination. A super duo who will smash many more records with the Seven Barrows brigade before they have finished.

9. 'He's a nice boy, rides some nice horses'

A casual conversation over a snooker table at Frenchie Nicholson's Cheltenham home was the first Pat Eddery knew that Peter Walwyn wanted him as first jockey to succeed Duncan Keith. 'I can remember the night very well,' says Pat. 'Mr Nicholson asked me to pop round to his home and then as we played snooker he told me that Peter Walwyn wanted me to join him. I was thrilled and, of course, I have not regretted the move in any way.' Just as Walwyn speaks highly of his rider, so, too, Pat is full of praise for the man he always describes as 'the guv'nor'. The Walwyn-Eddery link-up started in true fairy-tale style. Says Pat: 'The first ride I ever had for the guv'nor turned out to be a winner. I rode Silly Symphony for him at Wolverhampton in September, 1971. We set off in front and I made all the running to win by 1½ lengths. I rode for him a couple more times that season but Silly Symphony was the only winner. I was offered the job just before the August Bank Holiday. My first ride for him was at Epsom and again I won on Silly Symphony. But it was very close and I only beat Frankie Durr on Still Room by a neck.'

Silly Symphony was the first Walwyn-Eddery winner but their racing marriage has brought music to the ears of many gleeful punters. Silly Symphony was a daughter of Silly Season and here again there is a touch of irony as the first Classic horse Pat rode for the Seven Barrows team was also by Silly Season. His name was Lunchtime and at the end of the 1972 season, when he had been unbeaten in three outings, he did seem a really promising contender for the following season's Classics. Lunchtime was owned by Lt-Col Dick

Poole, who had been one of Walwyn's first patrons. He told me: 'I was a great friend of the Johnson Houghton family when Peter Walwyn held their licence for them. When he branched out on his own I sent him a couple of horses, although they were not very good. Golden Wedding, Lunchtime's dam, belonged to a cousin of mine. Lunchtime, who was her first foal, was part of the family, so to speak.'

Lunchtime, who was a tall, good looking colt, made his debut in the Goldings Maiden Stakes at Goodwood on September 12th, 1972. He ran out a very easy five lengths winner from Kambalda, who was also having his first ever outing. Kambalda, of course, went on to become a useful stayer. Lunchtime's performances at home must have whispered to the course because he started that day as a very warm 11–10 on favourite. When he won the Clarence House Stakes at Ascot by four lengths just nine days later he was already being talked about as a possible winter favourite for the following year's 2,000 Guineas. When he won the Dewhurst Stakes by 2½ lengths at Newmarket on October 13th his position was further consolidated. Says Pat: 'Make no mistake, he was possibly the best two-year-old I ever rode. He was a great two-year-old and a hell of a horse. What was so disappointing about him was that racegoers never even then saw him at his best because he always worked like lightning at home. He was top-class but even better at home on the gallops.' With these three victories behind him Lunchtime was allotted 9 st 2 lb in the Tote Free Handicap. Only the filly Jacinth and the Bernard Van Cutsem duo, Noble Decree (9–7) and Ksar (9–3), were rated higher. But amazingly Lunchtime never won another race in his career.

Said Dick Poole: 'Having been unbeaten as a two-year-old and winter favourite for the 2,000 Guineas he was a huge disappointment as a three-year-old.' When Peter Walwyn was forced to run Grundy in the Greenham Stakes he did so with in-built horror of the race. It was probably the experience with Lunchtime which started these fears. Lunchtime, seen as England's best hope of thwarting the Vincent O'Brien Classic raid with Thatch, was backed down to 11–4 on for the Greenham on April 14th. But it was to be a disastrous event for Lunchtime and Eddery as they went down by a length to Boldboy, ridden by Joe Mercer. Says Pat: 'Even after that defeat, which was his first run of the season, I still thought that he would win the 2,000 Guineas. But instead he finished nearly last. On his two-year-old form he must surely have won.' This was the shock 50–1 win of Mon Fils, who in fact had finished third, one length behind Lunchtime in the Greenham. It was a dream come true for his young trainer Richard Hannon, who suffered the cruel blow of having the horse taken from his yard after Mon Fils had run badly in the Derby. But after the Guineas a beaming Hannon exclaimed: 'I now have a meal ticket for life.' Hannon was certain that in the soft going his colt would run well. Visiting Clive Brittain at his yard on the very morning of the race Hannon said: 'Lend me fifty quid will you, Clive? I must nip down to the town and buy a new suit as I cannot possibly be seen in the winners' enclosure after the 2,000 Guineas with this old one.' Hannon was quite correct and, complete with new suit, welcomed Frankie Durr and Mon Fils back to the winners' enclosure. Lunchtime, who had every chance in running, finished sixteenth of the eighteen runners. He had just one more race in his life, the Predominate Stakes at Goodwood on May 16th, after which he went to stud. At Goodwood he was fitted with blinkers but these did little to improve his form and he finished a well-beaten fourth of nine behind Buoy. Said Dick Poole: 'After the Goodwood race it was obvious that the horse was not himself. He had been a great disappointment but we had him checked and it was found that he was over-producing the adrenalin in his body, which caused the pacemaker of his heart not to function properly when he was racing. He was sent to stud in Australia and is doing well in New South Wales.' Says Pat sadly: 'He could have been a really super horse. As a two-year-old he was a world-beater in his three races and at home he was even better.'

If Pat's hopes of a Classic win were boosted by the two-year-old form of Lunchtime he also had similiar encouragement from the grey colt Habat in his early days. But like

Lunchtime he proved a big disappointment as a three-year-old. Says Pat: 'I rated him pretty highly. But he was nothing like as good as Grundy. He won like a real good 'un at Ascot in the start of his three-year-old career but he then ran badly in the 2,000 Guineas and after that we had a bit of trouble with him.' Habat, owned by Mr Grundy himself, Carlo Vittadini, was pipped by a head in his first race, the Portsmouth Road Maiden Stakes at Kempton on May 29th, 1973. That day he was just beaten by Cyril Stein's Dragonara Palace, another grey colt who was named after Ladbrokes' string of Dragonara hotels. At Newbury on June 13th Habat was backed down to 2–1 on and duly won the Berkshire Stakes with Eddery on board by an easy five lengths. This win prompted Walwyn to think that Habat was well up to international two-year-old class and he next ran in the Prix Robert Papin at Maisons-Laffitte on July 29th. This was not a successful venture as Habat finished sixth behind Daniel Wildenstein's Lianga, who later in her career was finally to break the millionaire's 30-year winless hoodoo in England. But two more easy wins that autumn promoted Habat, like Lunchtime, to the top class of the English two-year-olds. In the Mill Reef Stakes at Newbury on September 8th he simply waltzed away from Boldini to win by five lengths and he showed his class that day because he easily beat the subsequent useful sprinter Bay Express. When he won the William Hill Middle Park Stakes by $2\frac{1}{2}$ lengths from Pitcairn at Newmarket on October 4th he had done all that could possibly be asked of him in his final two races. But *Raceform*'s John Sharratt was not totally impressed by Habat's Middle Park win. He recorded: 'Although he ran on better than Pitcairn, once in a clear lead, it was a workmanlike rather than impressive performance.' Habat was rated 9 st 1 lb in the Tote Free Handicap, which was the top English-trained colt. Apalachee, the massive Vincent O'Brien trained colt, had gone from last to first in the *Observer* Gold Cup to make the others look like hacks. Unbeaten in three races, this son of Round Table was allotted 9 st 7 lb in the Free Handicap. He was followed by the French-trained Mississipian with 9–2, while Apalachee's stable-companion Cellini, who won the

Dewhurst Stakes, was on the same mark as Habat with 9 st 1 lb.

Lunchtime never won a race as a three-year-old but Habat did win one. All winter he was quoted as third favourite for the 2,000 Guineas behind Apalachee and Cellini. And his first race as a three-year-old is the one which Eddery remembers well. They won the Ascot 2,000 Guineas Trial so impressively on April 6th, 1974 that the Irishman was convinced that he had a chance at Newmarket. But the writing was on the wall for Habat a long way from home in the 2,000 Guineas on May 4th. He eventually finished sixth behind the French-trained winner Nonoalco with Giacometti second. John Sharratt wrote at the time: 'Habat, under severe pressure at least two furlongs from home, never looked likely to get on terms. It is doubtful whether he gets the trip in top company.' Habat only had one more race in his career. He ran creditably in the Sussex Stakes at Goodwood on July 31st considering his long lay off. That day he was beaten two lengths by Ace of Aces, the Maurice Zilber-trained colt who had previously been employed as the pacemaker for Dahlia. It was shortly after this race that talks took place between Vittadini, his racing manager Keith Freeman, Peter Walwyn and Lt-Col Douglas Gray of the National Stud, where Habat now stands. For Walwyn the three-year-old career of Habat, like Lunchtime, was a bitter blow. But it was not long before he had an unbeaten two-year-old colt who went on to attain the dizzy heights of Classic glory.

Habat, a terrier-like grey with good acceleration in the Trial at Ascot, was not the only flop in the Guineas. Apalachee, hailed in Ireland as the greatest horse of all time and the fastest mover seen in Cashel since the first E-type whizzed through the village, was a complete disaster. Another reputation also went flying out of the window or rather across Newmarket Heath. Just before the Guineas I asked Ryan Price if he thought Giacometti was the best of our colts. 'Our best? *The* best, you . . . ! This is a great horse, don't you know?' Even after his defeats in three Classics – he was placed in the Guineas, Derby and St Leger – Price still maintained that he was a good horse and his opinion was finally vindicated in the Champion Stakes. He once told me: 'I am going to make a lot of people eat their words about this horse before I die.'

Ask Pat Eddery which is the best he has ever ridden and he naturally answers 'Grundy'. But ask him which is the next best horse he has partnered and he comes out with the answer just as quickly – 'Polygamy'. She was the filly who gave Pat his first ever Classic win in 1974 when she won the Oaks at Epsom. She was owned by one of the most successful owners in recent years, Louis Freedman. It was only in 1963 that Freedman first became actively interested in racing but he has enjoyed more success in this short time as an owner than most people have in a lifetime. He told me: 'I was always very interested in horses and racing. But it was only in 1963 that I decided to take the plunge and own my own horses. Quite honestly I thought it would be a once and for all venture. I imagined that I would buy two yearlings, keep them for a maximum of three years and then sell them and get out of the sport. But I was lucky in that I bought successfully, or rather the late Walter Nightingall bought wisely for me. At that stage of my racing career I was keen to have stayers rather than sprinters. It was the long distance races which were far more attractive to me. Now, of course, I am interested in breeding so it has to be the sprinter side which one concentrates on. Walter Nightingall went to Newmarket and bought two horses for me – French Wolf for 2000 guineas and I Say for 2500 guineas. Call it luck or good judgement but I Say was third in the English Derby in 1965 behind Sea Bird II and won the Coronation Cup the following year. I had never intended going into the breeding side but I then decided to keep I Say as a stallion and sent one or two mares to him.' It was in 1966 that Freedman, a wealthy London-based businessman, purchased the Cliveden Stud at Taplow, near Maidenhead in Berks. The stud was actually founded in 1906 by Lord Astor. Breeding his own horses Freedman immediately struck gold and he decided to send Seventh Bride and Lucyrowe to Peter Walwyn at the start of their three-year-old careers. Recalls Freedman: 'I was very impressed with the way Peter Walwyn was shooting up the ladder and was keen to have horses with him when Walter Nightingall died.'

Lucyrowe won the Ebbisham Stakes, Coronation Stakes, Nassau Stakes and Sun Chariot Stakes and was a top-class filly. Seventh Bride won the Princess Royal Stakes. Freedman also bought the Beech House Stud from the Sassoon Studs. This Newmarket-based stud was then sold in 1975 to Dr Carlo Vittadini. Freedman, who has close links too with Noel Murless, has also owned some top-class performers like Attica Meli (Yorkshire Oaks, Park Hill Stakes, Princess Royal Stakes). But it was Polygamy who really impressed Eddery. She was the daughter of Seventh Bride so the link with Seven Barrows and Walwyn was a close one. After being unplaced in her first race in 1973 Polgamy and Pat Eddery won the Princess Maiden Plate at Newmarket on July 4th. Ironically, the runner-up that day was the Queen's Highclere. Three lengths was Polygamy's winning margin but it was to be a different story when these two high-class fillies next galloped against each other across the famous Heath. After another two wins at headquarters Polygamy ended her two-year-old career with a creditable fourth in the Criterium des Pouliches at Longchamp, on the same day that Lester Piggott won the Arc de Triomphe on Rheingold.

On the same day at Ascot the following year as Habat enhanced his 2,000 Guineas claims with a Trial victory, Pat won on Polygamy in the fillies Trial. She ran out a very easy four lengths winner and was immediately made ante-post favourite for the 1,000 Guineas by all bookmakers.

'A real killer' is how Eddery describes the result of the photo finish in the 1,000 Guineas at Newmarket on May 2nd. He says: 'Polygamy was a great little mare. Believe me she was really good. After Grundy she was without doubt the best horse I have ever ridden. She was a lazy sort though and even when she won she did not look all that impressive.

'But as we went over the line in the 1,000 Guineas I was bloody certain that I had beaten Joe Mercer on the Queen's Highclere. It really was a killer when they announced the result the other way round. I couldn't believe it until I actually saw the photograph. I thought that if ever there was a certain result of a photo this was it. I definitely thought I had done it. I was especially keen as it would have been my first Classic winner. That day, like most times, she ran very, very lazy. I was not in the best of positions but luckily I was able to get through to challenge. Two furlongs out I thought that I would trot up. Joe Mercer and Highclere came at me but a stride before the line I was ahead. The other filly must have just got up on the line and won it on the nod. I was really disappointed after the race as Polygamy, although being lazy as hell, had run a blinder. The previous year she had easily accounted for Highclere and I thought we were certain to do so again.'

Recalls Freedman: 'To be honest, as the two fillies flashed across the line I did not think that I had won. I knew that it was very close and I was just pleased that Polygamy had run so well. I know before the announcement of the photograph that I would willingly have settled for a dead-heat.'

While Walwyn and Eddery were obviously disappointed at the result there was joy and cheering everywhere else to salute the Queen's victory. When the announcer said: 'First number seven, Highclere,' the monarch's face was a picture of happiness and there is no doubt that this victory gave her, and all racegoers present, immense pleasure.

But if Polygamy was a little unlucky at Newmarket she certainly had the gods on her side in the Oaks at Epsom. For this was the fillies Classic where the then reigning champion jockey, Willie Carson, staged a private rodeo show on Dibidale. His bare-back riding of the Barry Hills-trained filly in the closing stages was certainly one of the feats of the century. But for the saddle slipping it is virtually certain that Dibidale would have won the Oaks and Pat Eddery would not have scored his first Classic win on Polygamy, who was 3–1 favourite. Admits Pat: 'Maybe I was a little lucky but that was her race, she was prepared for it and gave me everything she had.' At the winning post Polygamy won by a length from Furioso with Dibidale half a length away in third place. But Dibidale was disqualified from third place because Carson was unable to draw the correct weight. He said after this remarkable race: 'Coming down Tatten-

Coup de Feu and Eddery go to post for their shock Eclipse Stakes win
1974. *(Below)* Charlie Bubbles striding out in the Newbury Spring
Cup in 1975 to give Eddery his 500th winner.

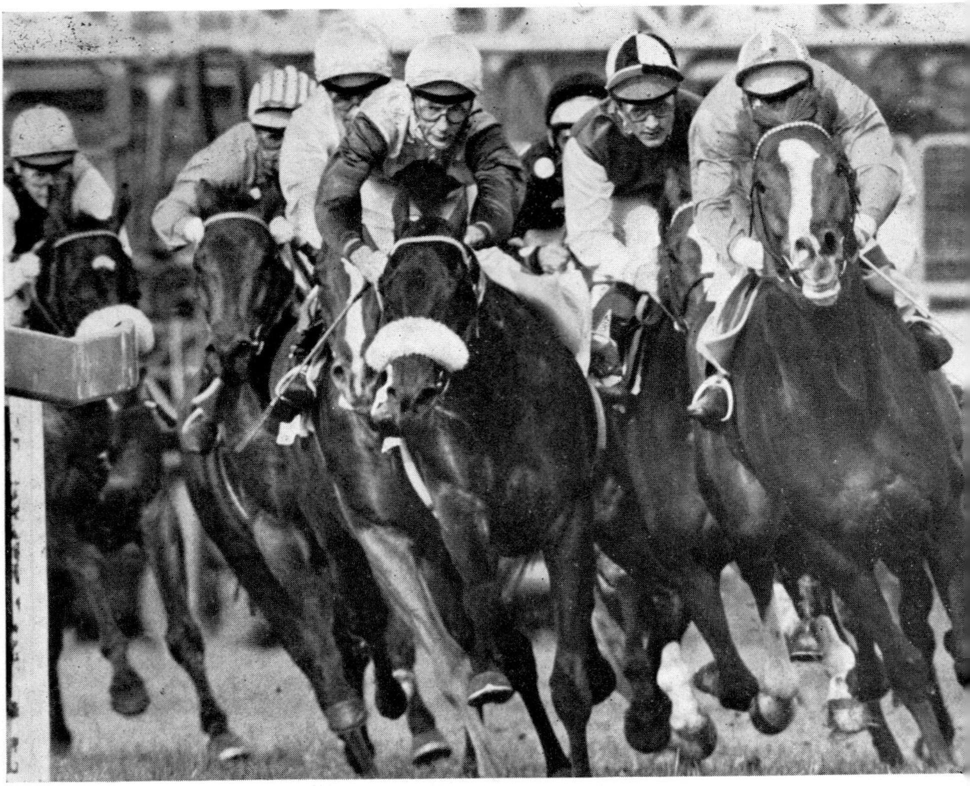

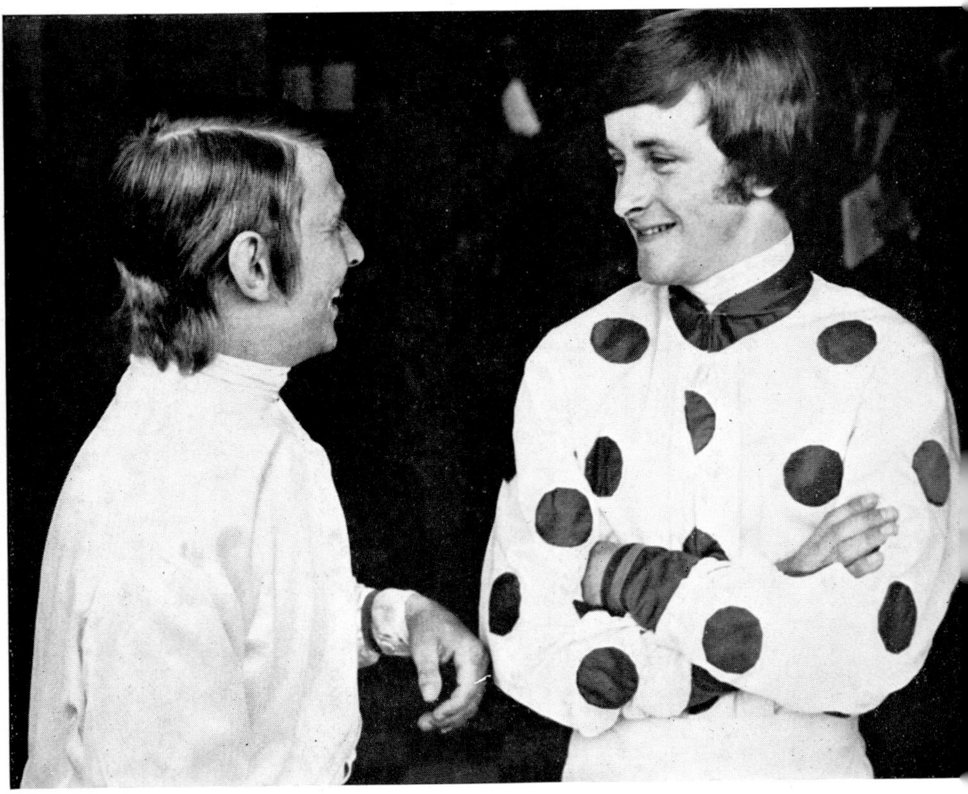

(*Opposite top*) Piggott and Eddery easily recognized in a hectic last bend dash at Sandown Park in 1975. (*Opposite below*) Willie Carson congratulates Eddery after the Irishman took his Champion Jockey title in 1974.

(*Right*) A mud-spattered Eddery gives an after-race verdict. (*Below*) Patch on his way to victory in the 1975 Lingfield Derby Trial.

Pat Eddery on Heavenly Form at Lingfield, showing all the dash and style of a champion, May 1974. *(Below)* A rare Lester Piggott smile as he congratulates the new champion after their tense battle for the title in 1974.

ham Hill I first realized that the saddle was slipping. In the next furlong we zoomed right up with the leaders and all the time it seemed as if the reins were getting longer and longer. I suppose I could have fallen off at any stage but it was not a time for being frightened. There is only one Oaks and I thought I might still have a chance if the weight cloth had stayed in the saddle.' Ignoring the flapping saddle round her loins, Carson kept riding. But first the weight cloth went adrift and then the number cloth. In the closing stages of the race, with Carson still riding like a demon, the saddle had slipped completely under the filly. Luckily Willie had kicked his feet out just in time. 'The greatest piece of riding I have ever seen,' said Brian Taylor, who only three days earlier had won his first Derby on Snow Knight. Eric Eldin, who tracked Carson on Northern Gem said: 'Even when the lot had gone, the little devil was still riding for his life.' It was cruel luck for Barry Hills, who only two years previously had seen the Derby snatched from his grasp by inches when Roberto just pipped his Rheingold. Little wonder that when he was planning his Derby riding arangements two years later he said dejectedly: 'Epsom doesn't seem to be my course.' On the very morning of the Dibidale incident Hills and the filly's owner, Nick Robinson, had decided not to risk her on the hard ground as her long term objective was always the Arc de Triomphe. But at six o'clock on the morning of the race a friend awoke Robinson from his slumbers and told him that it was raining heavily at Epsom and he should run the filly. Hills told everybody before the race: 'Only an act of God can stop Dibidale from winning.' After the race he must have thought that someone above was against him. Dibidale's misfortunes took some of the limelight away from Polygamy's win. Carson added: 'But for the saddle slipping underneath her belly Dibidale would have won half the track.' But Eddery claims: 'You would have had to shoot Polygamy to stop her.'

Peter Walwyn, gaining his second Classic triumph, was thrilled by the win, especially after the agonizing last-gasp defeat in the 1,000 Guineas. He said: 'Polygamy battles on. She is as tough as old boots. This was Pat's first Classic winner but it definitely will not be his last. Polygamy is like a tiger – a benevolent tiger. You'll never see a gamer filly.' Pat agrees: 'I was flat to the boards all the way and she was never really going well. But she does not know what it is to give up trying. Courage alone won her the race.' Owner Louis Freedman is full of praise for Eddery's handling of his filly. He said: 'She was the lazy type and Pat had to work on her after only one or two furlongs.'

The Queen's filly Escorial, who promised so much earlier in the season at York, was a complete flop and only beat two. Lester Piggott summed up the lack-lustre display in his own terse fashion: 'Didn't come down the hill, and didn't stay.'

When the Polygamy-Dibidale replay was staged in the Irish Guinness Oaks at the Curragh in July the latter was provided with a special breast-plate, usually used by steeplechasers. Said Hills: 'That accident at Epsom could well have been caused because Dibidale jumped across a path at Tattenham Hill. This time we are taking no chances.' For this, the twelfth running of the Guinness Oaks, Pat was attempting to follow his father Jimmy, who won a non-sponsored Oaks on Silken Glider in 1957.

On the basis of the way Dibidale ran away with the Curragh Classic by five lengths from Gaily it must be imagined that she, too, would have taken the Epsom equivalent but for the saddle incident. She was very impressive that day and Polygamy was relegated to third place with Furioso fourth. Says Eddery: 'She had definitely lost a little bit of her sparkle in Ireland and I think she was a bit stale after the Epsom race.'

Polygamy went to stud later in the season and never raced again. When I mentioned to Freedman that she was probably a lucky Oaks winner he quickly, and understandably, observed: 'She may have been. But she was not very lucky afterwards.' He was referring to her tragic death at stud, which means that we will never see the offsprings of Pat's first Classic winner. Still, Freedman has made great strides as an owner in racing in a short time. He admits: 'I think that the luck tends to level itself out. I certainly was not very lucky when the mare died.' When I asked him why he has succeeded as an owner where countless men have failed he replied: 'I think that you could say that I have had luck when I wanted it most. I seemed to have been associated with people in racing who have been extremely enthusiastic and that makes a great deal of difference.'

By the start of the 1974 Flat season Eddery was rated among the tip-top jockeys. But the year before it had been hinted that he might have had an outsider's chance for the title. He was still only twenty-one and told pressmen: 'It's nice of people to think that I could be that good. But anyone backing me to be champion this year or next must be stupid. If I finish in the top four it would be fantastic because it would mean that I have ridden 100 winners for the first time in a season. No, Lester Piggott is still the greatest for me. He may no longer be champion – Willie Carson is – but I think all the others of us are a long way behind him. Some of us may ride nearly as well but he is far more cunning. A great race rider.' By the end of the 1973 season Pat's hopes still rested on the then unbeaten Lunchtime. He said: 'He has a superb action. When you ride him it's like sitting in mid-air. He takes one stride to every horse's two. Although he was a big backward baby in all his three two-year-old races he won as he liked.' Far from disgraced, Eddery finished third in the jockeys' list in 1973 with 119 winners from 666 rides. Carson retained the title with 163 winners but with a much higher percentage of winners per rides Piggott was second with 129 wins.

At the start of the 1974 season it was hardly surprising that Corals offered: 11–8 on Carson, 6–4 Piggott, 8–1 Eddery about the championship. But the Walwyn-Eddery duo were quickly into top gear when their first runner, Tudor Rhythm, won at Doncaster on the second day of the Flat. Then the Seven Barrows stars maintained a hundred-per-cent win record when Paper Palace won at Doncaster on Lincoln day. Pat had finished well down the field in the Lincoln on Grasp Saint, who was trained by Fulke Johnson Houghton. But it was clear that the Walwyn team were in good shape as early as this in the season. By the end of April, Eddery's odds for the title had been clipped down to 4–1. With four winners from only seven mounts Eddery gave an early warning of what was to come. When Tilario won at Leicester on April 26th he was leader in the current list with four winners.

The same day champion Carson finally got off the mark when Mallane won. He was to be behind Eddery for the rest of the season. Pat always headed Carson, although Piggott did lead for a period. By the end of May Eddery had scored twenty winners and my press colleague John Trickett described it aptly when he wrote: 'A waterfall of winners is cascading through his hands.' By now Eddery was only a 2–1 shot for the title and he admitted: 'I've never had a start to the season like this. It's unbelievable, fantastic. My stable horses have been running so well and everything has been going my way. I feel I must have a little chance of the title. I am getting plenty of rides – and that's the most important thing. Mind you, so is Willie Carson. When he gets the breaks he will be a hard man to beat.'

It was soon clear that it was a three-man race for the title. Eddery, still only twenty-two but a perfect horseman, Carson, the never-give-up Scotsman and the Long Fella himself. Carson has done so well to reach the top. He was once in a car crash and as he lay on the side of the motorway with crumpled metal and splintered glass all around him he heard two ambulance men say: 'Don't worry about him, he's a bloody goner.'

With the Oaks win of Polygamy making up for the disappointing Guineas performances of the same filly and Habat, all was now set for the highlight of the racing year – Royal Ascot, the champagne sipping, lobster guzzling Royal party which always brings together the best horses. But the top-hatted turn-out was to be a disaster for Pat. In the very first race on the card, the £5000 Queen Anne Stakes, there was a complete sensation with three jockeys being stood down for 'careless and improper riding'. Confusion (Greville Starkey), Gloss (Pat Eddery) and Royal Prerogative (Mickey Goreham) finished first, second and third – and were then all disqualified. The race was awarded to the grey Italian raider Brook, who had finished fourth nearly ten lengths behind the aptly named Confusion.

As Pat's ban was due to start on June 27th it was clear that he would miss the ride on English Prince in the Irish Sweeps Derby at the Curragh on June 29th. This was seen as a great chance for English Prince, who had not raced as a two-year-old but had simply trotted up in the Predominate Stakes at Goodwood by six lengths. He missed the Epsom Derby but after the shock win of Snow Knight was widely considered to be the best three-year-old colt in England. When he won the King Edward VII Stakes at Royal Ascot it was obvious that the home-bred Hue-Williams colt was extremely good. It was hard for Eddery to suffer the ban. He was not the leading offender in the Queen Anne rumpus. It was a case of 'six of one and half a dozen of the other'. Pat won on English Prince knowing that he would be unable to have the Curragh ride. In fact he never won on English Prince again as when he had his last race the duo were well beaten by Bustino in the Great Voltiguer at York. Said Eddery after the Confusion race: 'I was the one who should have got the race, not ended up being banned. I went for a hole and I was just unlucky that it closed on me. I am sick – especially as Brook is a right villain of a horse and nearly killed Tony Murray when he rode him in Italy last season.' It was the first time in racing history that the first three past the post were all disqualified for careless riding by their jockeys. Initially Eddery objected to Confusion. Then Brook's jockey Brian Taylor objected to Eddery for 'taking my ground one furlong out'. It was the first ever Royal Ascot ride for Australian Mickey Goreham, who was on the 6–4 'hot-pot' Royal Prerogative. Brook was owned by Dr Carlo Vittadini. His luck was never more evident than on that day as Brook's only previous run in England was when he had finished last in the Lockinge Stakes at Newbury.

Robbed of the ride in the Irish Derby, Eddery was indeed a sad man. At this time he was in absolutely brilliant form. He ended Royal Ascot with forty-five winners for the season – way ahead of his total the previous year when he did not get his half century until mid-July. Punters who had backed Carson to keep the title were already taking sleeping tablets.

For Walwyn the problem was who would replace Pat in Ireland. Lester Piggott was an obvious choice and talks did take place about the possibility of him taking over. But then Lester said: 'I have one or two more options open,' and in his usual way was not prepared to be tied down for the mount. Walwyn was swift to act. He immediately contacted Yves Saint-Martin and it was arranged that the idol of Paris would have the ride. Having lost Eddery, and been kept waiting by Piggott, Walwyn did the wisest thing and engaged the talented Frenchman. It must have been heartbreaking for Eddery to watch English Prince skate home at the Curragh with Yves on top by 1½ lengths from Imperial Prince, who was also owned by the Hue-Williams family. Just prior to Royal Ascot Pat had showed his best form and had ridden ten winners in only five days. By missing the ride on English Prince Eddery lost his £6000 percentage. When he went back to the Curragh and could only finish third on Polygamy in the Irish Oaks his agony was complete.

But in England there was no stopping him. By mid-August he was odds-on favourite for the title. He went to the big York meeting at the peak of his form. Eleven winners had come his way in the previous four days – five of them in successive rides at Newbury on the Saturday and Leicester on the Monday. On the brink of his second century Eddery admitted: 'Even now I don't believe that I will do it. There is still a long way to go. It's the first time that I have looked like being champion. It's all right for Lester, he has been at the top for years and knows all the pressures. You have got to be lucky and it did not do me any good when we closed our stable down for a week because of the virus.' Walwyn, so skilful in placing horses, was behind Eddery all the way and even at this stage of the season said: 'We have a lively bunch of two-year-olds you have not really seen yet.' That was the understatement of the season.

On August 18th in clinging mud at Newbury Eddery rode a three-timer on Realistic, Pericet and Gaelic to take his score to ninety-six, only six at this stage behind Lester Piggott, who had previously had one of his unique spells when one thought that he could have won any race, anywhere. One sensed that the old maestro was really hunting the title he lost to Carson and some of his all-powerful, driving finishes had to be seen to be believed. It was Lester at his best, riding like a man possessed. Ragstone, who had won the previous seven consecutive races for the Duke of Norfolk, hated the clinging Newbury going and was well beaten into third place behind Pat on the front-running Realistic.

Eddery's luck had been out at York and but for the Newbury treble he had been having a quiet time. But at Goodwood on August 23rd he reached the magic century with a double on two chance mounts, Cesarewitch hope Reine Beau and Phlox. Alan Bond had enjoyed four successive wins on Reine Beau for Mick Masson but had injured himself at Brighton. The progressive stayer was seen at his best in the Bentinck Stakes, although it looked as though the runaway little Eric had stolen the race with a long lead. But Eddery timed his run to perfection and came storming through to catch Eric and win by half a length. Eddery then replaced Lester Piggott, who was riding at Newmarket, and he made it 100 winners when he won on Phlox. Even then Eddery refused to admit that he could topple Piggott, who kept up his challenge by taking his score to 111 with Magnum Force at Newmarket. 'Lester has it buttoned up,' claimed Pat on the day of his century achievement.

The lead of Lester was reduced to eight when Eddery won on Pollinella at Chepstow on August 27th. But the same day Piggott won on Bombshell at Epsom. It was obvious that it was to be a desperately close battle for the title. At Chepstow Walwyn said: 'All my horses have recovered from the virus and are running well. I have a lot of good two-year-olds who have not run yet. I still think that Pat has a reasonable chance of winning the championship.' Frenchie Nicholson observed wisely: 'It's going to be tough but Pat doesn't worry much about it. His weight – 7 lb less than Lester – will tell in the end. But don't forget that Lester has connections with every stable in the land. All the big stables use him, apart from Peter Walwyn, and this means he can pick the best. He is also the best judge of form in the country and knows what he should ride. Even so, I think Pat will be the champion.'

A stomach upset meant that Lester had to forgo four rides at Brighton the next day. In his absence Eddery closed the gap with a double at Haydock. At the end of August the score was Piggott 115, Eddery 109. But by September 3rd Eddery was only three behind, after Hello Honey had obliged at Brighton. At this time Lester was riding in France on several occasions and these quick trips across the Channel did not enhance his chances.

By September 9th Eddery had gone seven clear of Piggott and was rated as 4–1 on for the title. Lester was out of action at York because of a slight chill and one of Pat's double was on a ride he inherited from Lester, Doubt Me Not. A day later Ladbrokes made both Eddery and Piggott odds-on for the title. 'We go 5–6 and take your pick,' said a Ladbrokes spokesman, who added that Edward Hide, the third century maker of the season, was 33–1 to upset the apple-cart. With nine weeks to go it was a two-man race but already the Walwyn battery of star two-year-olds were beginning to speed into various winners' enclosures. Grundy had emerged on the scene and when the Eddery-Grundy team won the Champagne Stakes at Doncaster on September 11th it meant that the Irishman had gone two clear of Piggott. No opening appeared for Grundy until the closing stages but Eddery sat still, waited with the utmost patience, and then made him run. He was certainly riding like a champion, even if he did not officially wear the crown. With his score at 121 Eddery was two ahead – but Piggott was then 11–10 on with some bookmakers for the title. Lester was still determined to achieve his tenth champion success.

After Grundy's success Walwyn provided Pat with a three-timer at Goodwood on September 13th. By September 21st he had stretched the lead out to five. Every day was a fascinating duel between the two of them searching for winners, often miles across the country at different meetings. At Newbury Pat had another double while Lester could only score one at Ayr. At this stage Ladbrokes went 13–8 on Eddery, 5–4 Piggott. A blank at Ayr and Eddery weighed in with a Yarmouth double. It was then 6–4 on Eddery, 11–10 Piggott. The gap was still five after Pat notched a double and Lester a single. Excitement was really mounting. Towards the end of September the picture became more clear. Lester flew to Ireland, only to draw a blank, but Pat had a weekend double and the score on September 23rd was Eddery 132, Piggott 125. It was then 3-1 on Eddery and 5-2 Piggott.

With just ten days to go the Irishman was seven ahead. He turned down the chance of riding in the Washington International on his Eclipse winner, Coup de Feu, so that he would not miss a single day's racing in England. While the winners were still flowing in for Eddery, Walwyn was greatly enhancing his chances of reaching the magic century. No trainer in England had achieved this since Bill Elsey's grandfather, William, had a total of 124 wins in 1925. By November 4th, on the eve of Lester's 39th birthday, the lead was six and it seemed that this would be enough to ensure that Pat won the title. Both had a winner at Lingfield on this day. Lester's chances were reduced when he elected to ride Dahlia in the Washington International, a slightly wasted trip as the great mare finished third behind Admetus. Eddery did not miss out on Coup de Feu who came sixth ridden by Sandy Barclay.

When I contacted Walwyn about the plans for his two-year-olds about a month previously he joked: 'I must keep firing the ammunition to make Pat champion.' All the plans for his star juveniles like Grundy, No Alimony, Corby, Consol and Record Token were arranged to perfection. He carefully worked his way through the Racing Calendar and was able to find races for them without ever clashing, thereby giving Pat the chance for more winners. He had his autumn programme for his two-year-olds and if he had not done his job so well I doubt if Eddery could have been champion. When I chatted with Eddery just before the annual finale trip to Haydock, he admitted for the very first time that year: 'I think I must do it now, surely I will. It means that Lester has got to ride about four winners a day. If anybody can, he can. But I have got to fancy my chances now.' I asked Pat what discussions he and Lester had about the neck-and-neck title race they had staged all season. He said: 'Nothing. That would be the last thing Lester would ever talk about. We have never once talked about the title. Lester doesn't talk about that sort of thing. After I have won a race he may say "Well done" but that's as far as it goes.'

The last rounds of this thriller were staged at Haydock. On the opening day of the final two-day meeting Lester scored a double on Unicorn's Fancy and Sailing Ship. Pat took a rare day off and so the scene was set for the grand finale.

The head-on clash between two riders, so totally different in style and character, was now to reach boiling point. If Harry Levene had promoted the last round he could not have done it better. Lester needed to win five races to snatch the crown from young Pat's grasp.

Impossible? Probably, but the bookies were only prepared to offer 50–1 against Lester performing a magic trick. As Eddery was driven by brother-in-law Terry Ellis from his Manchester hotel, seventeen miles away, to Haydock on a rain-lashed near-winter day, his mind went back to August 22nd, 1970 – the day he, as an almost unknown apprentice, had ridden five winners at Haydock Park. Now the old master needed a similiar effort to rob Pat of his moment of glory. When he arrived at the course, with autumn leaves already fluttering down and punters quick-stepping it under cover for shelter, Pat said: 'I will not think about myself being champion until the last race has been run. I know that most people think that I am the champion but I certainly don't . . . yet. If I can ride five winners here as an apprentice I am sure Lester can, and he has got some fancied rides.' For Eddery the excitement of it all could be seen in his eager face and twinkling eyes. Having been pestered by the press and television for months he was now a little more relaxed. He knew that barring a miracle he could be the champion. The champagne in the weighing-room had already been ordered.

Only one man could cause the bubbles to go flat. Only a miracle could stop Pat now. But it did not happen.

Lester for whom the excitement, press interviews and television cameras were distinctly old hat, rode his first ever winner at Haydock some twenty-six years previously – four years before Eddery was even born. Now his first ride Bold

Sage in the opening race was backed down to 15–8 favourite but could only finish third. It meant that Lester could not be outright champion. Neither of the two stars rode in the next race but the Vernon's Sprint Cup decided the issue. Pat finished sixth on Talk of the Town but Lester was ninth on Sarasota Star and that clinched it because it meant that he could not overhaul Pat. When Pat led every inch of the way in the final race of the season, the Conclusion Stakes, on Pierino, he took his score to 148, five in front of Lester. Hide ended with 137 and the ex-champion Carson had 129. At twenty-two Pat became the youngest champion since Gordon Richards first landed the title in 1925. Said Pat of the Vernon Sprint: 'I knew that I was champion when I never saw Lester throughout the race. I must admit that I was keeping an eye out for him nearly as closely as I was watching the leaders. I was so excited that I nearly forgot to weigh in.' Pressmen who wanted some quotes from Lester were in for a disappointment. All he ventured was: 'He's a nice boy and he rides some nice horses.' But when the two were photographed together the old Piggott countenance, once likened to a 'well kept grave', did crease into a rare and genuine smile.

Pat's success even produced a letter in *The Times*. A gentleman from Jersey wrote: 'Whilst in no way wishing to detract from the splendid achievement of Patrick Eddery in becoming the 1974 Flat Race Champion, the continued brilliance of Lester Piggott can be confirmed statistically. Piggott won 24.4 per cent of his races, whereas Eddery could only achieve first on 19.7 per cent of his mounts. At the same time, Piggott failed to get into the frame on only 47 per cent of his mounts, whereas Eddery was unplaced in over 53 per cent of his races.' Valid points but, of course, Lester was able to pick and choose his plum rides. He was not forced to ride for one stable, when obviously all the goods cannot be gilt-edged. But there were few snails in the Walwyn camp and he also had a magnificent season with ninety-six wins in England and enough abroad to top one hundred. Statistics can often lie but it is true that Eddery had 164 more rides than Piggott – for just five more wins.

By now Eddery's picture was not confined to the sports pages of the national newspapers. Gossip writers were in on the act. 'Britain's top jockey is first past the post, but he's yet to fall for a filly' was one heading. 'Britain's most eligible bachelor' was another heading to an article of similar vein. Being champion means that the press are never far away and I suspect Pat, a quiet-talking individual, could have done without all the blaze of publicity. Still, he overcame the approaches in typically courteous fashion and I know of few journalists who have ever had anything but a warm response to their questions. Like the horse he rode when he won the title Pat became the Talk of the Town.

Said Pat: 'It was only when I overtook Lester for the last time that I realized the terrible strain. But you have got to accept these pressures at the top. It was worst when people kept coming up to me and talking as though it was all over and I was the champion.'

Within two weeks Pat was in South Africa, bound for a season in Hong Kong. A year later he followed the same pattern and joked to me: 'You have got to earn the money while you can, you know.' When he talks he speaks intently, often carefully selecting his words. He has an engaging grin and one feels that while a conversation is taking place he is carefully chewing over its contents.

One of the big races in South Africa, the Natal Fillies Guineas at Pietermaritzburg saw those jockeys fight out a thrilling finish . . . Eddery and Piggott. It was Pat who won by a short head on Forever Amber from Lester on Faerie Queen. Both fillies were trained by Fred Rickaby, brother of former English jockey, Bill Rickaby, and a cousin of Lester.

So the English season which ended on a rainy day at Haydock still had a link with a fillies Classic thousands of miles away in sunny South Africa. But the result, as with the 1974 championship, was still the same.

Eddery first, Piggott second.

10. 'I didn't have a prayer'

If ever a Pat Eddery Fan Club is formed it is a racing certainty that young Lambourn trainer Duncan Sasse will be President – probably Chairman as well. For no trainer has a higher regard for Eddery. Duncan and I were once discussing the top jockeys and he went as far as to say: 'I think Pat's better than Piggott. He makes fewer mistakes. I'd definitely prefer him of the two if I had to make a straight choice. I think that with almost any horse Pat will give him a perfect ride. He's a natural genius once he gets into the saddle.'

It is hardly surprising that Sasse has such a high regard for Eddery. When the fourth training winner of your career turns out to be the £38 000 Benson and Hedges Eclipse Stakes at Sandown the occasion and the jockey who steered the big race to glory are bound to be top of any popularity poll. Hailing from a keen racing family it was no surprise when Duncan decided to seek his career in the sport. He had a truly international grounding, working in Australia, America and France before returning to England. Then he joined Barry Hills at Lambourn and stayed there for three years until setting up in his own right as a trainer at Frenchman's Yard, Upper Lambourn at the start of the 1974 season. His father, Tim Sasse, is an expert on horse breeding and was the author of the book *Theme on a Pipedream*, which dealt with the breeding and statistics of Derby winners. Tim was one of the gilt-edged syndicate who purchased the majority share in Rheingold shortly before he came second in the 1972 Derby, just touched off by Roberto. Rheingold's Arc triumph and his successful syndication to stud for £1 million certainly proved a shrewd financial undertaking for Tim Sasse, Charles St George and other Lloyd's underwriters.

Having made the bold decision to start up as a trainer at the start of the 1974 season at the age of only twenty-three, Duncan had to obtain some useful horses – not only two-year-olds but older horses to start his string in business. Luckily for the Sasse brigade the much-respected Newmarket trainer Jack Watts, who sent out Indiana to win the St Leger in 1964, had decided to retire and was sending most of his horses to Newmarket sales. Among the horses who had been training, and were now for sale, was Coup de Feu.

Coup de Feu, a lengthy White Fire III colt, won twice for Watts as a two-year-old and on his reappearance as a three-year-old easily accounted for twenty-three rivals when giving weight all round in the race after Sovereign Bill had won the Lincoln at Doncaster. In seven runs later that season he gained just one more win. But in the Dante Stakes at York in May he was going very well in the closing stages and finished third, 5½ lengths behind Rheingold. As a four-year-old Coup de Feu failed to get into the winners' enclosure. In four races the nearest he obtained was a second behind the smart Scottish Rifle in the Westbury Stakes at Kempton in May. I suspect that the form behind Rheingold had been remembered by the Sasse family and when he entered the sales ring at Newmarket they were keen to buy him. Says Duncan: 'My father is very good on his breeding knowledge but it was Coup de Feu's past form more than anything else which attracted us. We thought that with a little bit of improvement he would win good races. He had already shown in his life that he had some ability.'

Tim Sasse purchased Coup de Feu for 26000 guineas and the horse joined his son with a small string of horses when he started on his own in 1974. On March 1st Coup de Feu had his first race for his new trainer when he finished second with Willie Carson on board at Cagnes-sur-Mer. Few British trainers can have started their careers with a first runner in the South of France.

On March 10th Coup de Feu finished fifth again at Cagnes-sur-Mer. The winner was My Brief, ridden by Tony Murray, and one of a group of horses sent on a long-distance raid by John Dunlop from Arundel. The horse to finish fourth that day was Star Appeal, another performer who was to steal Eclipse glory later on in his career. When Coup de Feu made his debut for Sasse in England he was beaten in an apprentices' race at Wolverhampton by Track Minstrel and the 26000 guineas investment did not appear to be the greatest snip of the century. But Lester Piggott steered the five-year-old home to win the Herring Daw Newbury Spring Cup and Coup de Feu obtained third place in the infamous Queen Anne Stakes, which will always be remembered for the sensational start to Royal Ascot when Pat Eddery (Gloss), Greville Starkey (Confusion) and Mick Goreham (Royal Prerogative) were all banned for four days for 'careless and improper riding'. This ban meant that Eddery was unable to ride English Prince in the Irish Derby at the Curragh on June 29th.

At this early stage of his training career, when he had registered three winners, Duncan was employing the best jockeys available. But he was striking up a happy partnership with Geoff Baxter, who was based handily near to his Lambourn stable and could ride out for him in the mornings. Tim Sasse takes up the most remarkable, and hitherto unpublished, part of Coup de Feu's Eclipse triumph. He says: 'After his improved form we were certainly keen to let him take his chance in the Eclipse Stakes. Geoff Baxter was offered the ride on him in the big race but turned him down flat because he had four booked, and fancied rides at Bath on the same afternoon. Looking round for a top jockey was not too easy as Lester was on Hail the Pirates and Willie Carson on Ksar. I found Pat Eddery outside a weighing-room a few days before the race and said: 'Will you ride Coup de Feu for me in the Eclipse?' I told him that I thought he had a good chance, was improving all the time and was bound to be in the first three. I can remember him looking back at me, laughing happily away like he does and saying "Do you really think so?" Anyway I convinced him that the horse had a squeak and he agreed to ride. The irony of the situation was that Coup de Feu hacked in and poor Geoff Baxter went to Bath and had two fourths and two unplaced. That's how unlucky you can be in racing.'

Admits Pat: 'I didn't think I had a prayer – no chance of winning whatsoever. Coup de Feu was 33–1 and that was about his chance. I don't think apart from the Classic wins, I have ever enjoyed a ride more. There was something special about winning a race when I honestly did not think I had a cat in hell's chance of even being in the first four. I simply jumped him off and he kept going like a little beauty. With the slow early pace of the race I was always able to keep pretty handy. I went second in the straight and then I realized that I had a great chance. I was hacking at the finish and nobody could get anywhere near me.'

Duncan Sasse says: 'He really thought he had no chance. I kept meeting him in the days prior to the race and he just laughed. Still he did not have a ride in the race so he was grateful for the offer. If I remember rightly it was the first time Pat had ever ridden for me and he had only had a little pipe opener on Coup de Feu at home.' Coup de Feu certainly lived up to his name in the race. His name is the French for pistol shot and he simply flew in like a high-speed bullet. Yet again there was another enormous gamble on Giacometti who had previously been second to Nonoalco in the 2,000 Guineas and third in the Epsom Derby behind Snow Knight. Tony Murray had the 3–1 favourite ideally placed but he was one of the first to come under pressure. It was Ksar who finally made second, three lengths behind Coup de Feu. Mount Hagen finished third, with Toujours Pret fourth for the second year running. Giacometti was fifth and Murray admitted 'No excuses'. Ryan Price, such a staunch admirer of Giacometti, said: 'He was absolutely bloody hacking two furlongs out when in two strides he choked up and stopped to nothing. He may have swallowed his tongue.' Averof was another huge disappointment, finishing tenth. Brian Taylor said: 'We were hammered when I came to make my run and he never settled as he did when he won so well at Royal Ascot.' At 33–1 Coup de Feu was the longest priced Eclipse winner for forty-three years. Says Duncan: 'I backed him each way as I thought he was bound to run really well.'

Eddery's personal bonanza from Coup de Feu's win was a £3000 cut which in some way made up for missing the £6000 prize he would have won if he had been able to ride English Prince in the Irish Derby the previous week. Coup de Feu joined the élite band of recent Eclipse winners like those two great rivals Mill Reef, who won as a three-year-old in 1971, and Brigadier Gerard, who won as a four-year-old in 1972. If somebody had been bold enough to venture the opinion in the joyous Sandown winners' enclosure that afternoon that Coup de Feu would never win another race in his life he would probably have received a real ear-bashing. But that is the way it turned out. He was subsequently third with Eddery on board behind Nonoalco at Deauville on August 11th. He was never running anything like his best in the Arc de Triomphe and only beat one – again ridden by Eddery – in Allez France's superb victory in the Paris spectacular. Later he was sixth in the Champion Stakes behind Giacometti and was ridden by Sandy Barclay in the Washington International at Laurel Park on November 9th when he was sixth behind Sir Michael Sobell's Admetus. He had a hard season but later went to California and that is where he broke down. Says Tim Sasse: 'I still believe firmly that he was much underrated. In 1975 he had an operation for a splintered bone and it was hoped to get him fit for Deauville. He obviously injured himself in California and that is why he ran so badly there in his three or four races. Anyway I am not sure he was suited for their greyhound style tracks.'

By the end of the 1975 Flat season in England, when Coup de Feu had not made an appearance, Duncan related sadly: 'He broke down and although he has improved he cannot possibly race again.' He was sent to the Aston Upthorpe Stud at Aston Tirrold, Berkshire, which is managed by colourful ex-jump jockey Dave Dick and houses Charles St George's Lorenzaccio. Before he finally went to the December Sales, Duncan told me: 'Nobody seems over keen to want him at this stage. He is by White Fire III, who was exported to Japan and nobody knows much about him and how he has done. Although he is a half-brother to Gallant Bid and St Leger winner Peleid nobody wants to know very much. It is annoying as he won the Eclipse so well. He absolutely hacked up and there can be no truth in the idea that he was just a fluke winner. He was very competitive and had lots of speed.'

Duncan is not exaggerating when he says that he regards Eddery as the very best jockey. He says: 'No matter what horse you give him he will give it the very best ride he can. He is only a few years away from being a really great jockey. I have never once given him a single race riding instruction. You always let him ride his own race. He has natural flair and to give him a load of orders might confuse him. As a rider he has so much natural ability. As a person he is totally unbiased and honest – and that is very important in a jockey. I don't think he is an extra brainy rider. He simply has a great deal of natural ability, rather like some of our top footballers. He picks things up quickly and the tremendous success he has achieved in a short time has not gone to his head. Now and again he feels he has to unwind and may shock a few people. But he has matured a hell of a lot. He gets on especially well with us younger trainers. He never has to call me sir and I would not expect it. I've heard it said that like other jockeys he doesn't readily buy the drinks but I have known him to be very generous after a good win. He will splash out and buy a lot of people dinner and bottles of champagne without blinking an eyelid. Like many top-class jockeys his life-style is so hectic. Six rides a day, sometimes seven days and two or three evenings a week. He gets very much involved in the racing scene. Funnily enough, when Coup de Feu won the Eclipse you would have expected us to have a riot. But we just had a quiet dinner and it was only a week later that it suddenly dawned on us what had happened and then we really celebrated. Having a big winner like that really drains you of all your energy. Like many other trainers we wait until we see if Peter Walwyn is running his horses in various races. We enter horses and hope that Peter will not run his. That gives us a chance to line up Pat. But Peter Walwyn has so many horses and often we have to take our horses out as we would rather not run than use another jockey.

'I'll tell you how good Pat is. I have a horse called Boulevardier. Pat is literally the only man who can ride him. It's that simple. There is all sorts of trouble unless Pat gets the ride. He is always keen to ride for me. Perhaps after Coup de Feu he thinks I have another no-hoper who may win a big race for him again!'

At the December Sales, 1975, Coup de Feu was sold to stud in Australia – just like Alvaro – and made 52000 guineas, exactly double the price Sasse paid for him.

11. The Great Grundy

It had to happen upon the lovingly prepared turf of Ascot's Royal heath. This was the perfect venue for the running of what was arguably the greatest horserace of all-time. The best cricket centuries should ideally be scored before a packed audience at Lord's. So, too, the 1975 running of the King George VI and Queen Elizabeth Diamond Stakes was the perfect setting for an unforgettable battle. This was the equine duel of the century between the previous year's St Leger winner, Bustino, and the great Grundy. It developed into a straight match between these two super stars and also a tactical battle between two outstanding jockeys. With twenty-eight years' riding experience behind him Joe Mercer received the leg up on Lady Beaverbrook's former 21 000 guineas yearling purchase. In the rival camp was Pat Eddery, barely twenty-three years old, on Grundy. But it was the Grundy-Eddery duo who stole the show with a display more sparkling than all the diamonds De Beers, the race sponsors, could ever hope to muster.

Like two boxers, dead level on points, Grundy and Bustino gave us a final round which will still be remembered and talked about at the turn of the century. Grundy and Eddery built up a partnership which was to shatter all records. In all Grundy won a staggering £312 122 in prize-money. Because of circumstances we never really knew how great he was. He won the English and Irish Derbys and produced a record time in the King George VI to hold off Bustino but we will never really be able to gauge how outstanding he was compared to other recent brilliant Derby winners such as Sir Ivor, Royal Palace, Nijinsky and Mill Reef. If a league table was compiled of these outstanding colts it would be hard to place them in the correct order. But despite an upset in his training routine at a vital time Grundy carved his name deeply into Turf history and whenever the victories of Grundy are recalled in years to come the name of Pat Eddery will share the limelight.

Judging how good two-year-olds will be the following year in their Classic careers is a far from easy task. But by the end of Grundy's two-year-old programme Pat was sure he had struck up a partnership with a potential world-beater. He told me: 'After Grundy had won the Dewhurst at New-market in the autumn of 1974 I was sure that I had ridden a colt of exceptional ability. Just after the Dewhurst I bought an Afghan puppy for £70. I couldn't think of what to call him but I already had tremendous respect for Grundy and reckoned he was going to be a good 'un. For this reason I called the dog Grundy.' A year after Pat had bought the dog, Grundy the horse had been retired to stud. But his achieve-ments as a three-year-old will grace every racing record book. Unbelievably Pat paid £70 for the Afghan puppy in 1974 – exactly twice as much as the great grand-dam of Grundy cost at the sales ring at Newmarket. The Grundy legend un-folds in the most modest way – with an old racing mare who was as slow as a snail.

Lundy Parrot was her name. She was the great grand-dam of Grundy but a more moderate racehorse you would be hard pressed to find for she definitely never won a race. But this is where the Grundy legend begins. In 1945, two mem-bers of the well-known Holland-Martin racing family – Ruby and Thurston – were setting up their own private stud at Overbury, Tewkesbury in Gloucestershire. Keen to secure some foundation mares they visited a dispersal sale at New-market. One of the lots was Lundy Parrot, who had been put in the sale by the executors of the late Lord Glanely. Says Tim Holland-Martin, who now owns the Overbury Stud: 'Two of my uncles paid the princely sum of thirty-five guineas for Lundy Parrot. Of course that could buy a few hot dinners in those days but it wasn't really very much money. There certainly is no trace of Lundy Parrot having won a race but she was to start the line straight through to Grundy. She was the foundation mare of our stud.'

Tim Holland-Martin took over the stud when an uncle died in January, 1968. 'I still bump around occasionally,' says Tim modestly but he is one of the more skilled amateur riders. 'I have ridden about fifty winners in all,' he told me before the start of the 1975-76 winter campaign. 'About twenty-four under rules, so I suppose I need just one more to lose my allowance! My best win was on that good mare Sally Furlong in the United Hunts at Cheltenham when the going was so heavy they had to switch the start of the race and also the Gold Cup and we actually kicked-off down the course. Like Pat Eddery, I started really with Frenchie Nicholson. He put up with me for a winter being run away with all over Cleeve Hill.

'Grundy was the second foal of Word from Lundy, who is one of our resident mares. She was a good racing sort, trained by Fulke Johnson Houghton, who won three races in her career – the Saddlecombe Stakes at Brighton as a two-year-old, the St George Stakes at Chester and the Royal County Handicap at Windsor as a three-year-old. In all she had ten races, won three times and was once placed as a three-year-old at Lingfield.' Fulke Johnson Houghton said: 'Word from Lundy was a good racing mare – nothing really special. She was a sturdy type of horse and was quite capable of staying two miles. Just before the Derby when there was all the talk about Grundy not staying the trip I was certain that he would. Word from Lundy ran over this distance without any trouble and I knew that Grundy was certain to get the $1\frac{1}{2}$ miles in the Derby because of his mother's performances.'

Says Tim: 'Our stud had a share in Great Nephew from a syndicate of some forty shares. Each year we had the nomination to send one mare to him at the Dalham Hall Stud at Newmarket. In his career Great Nephew won £40282 including the Prix du Moulin de Longchamp and the Prix Dollar. He was second in the 2,000 Guineas and Eclipse Stakes and was retired to stud in 1968.'

The Great Nephew-Word from Lundy mating took place at Newmarket but Grundy was actually born at the Wood-

134

park Stud, Dunboyne, County Meath in Ireland. His birth-day was April 3rd, 1972. Word from Lundy had gone to Ireland to be covered later by Tower Walk, who was resident at the Woodpark Stud, but ironically nothing transpired from the mating. So Word from Lundy's trip to Ireland was in some ways wasted. But there was nothing wrong with the young foal, who eventually returned to Overbury after three months.

Recalls Holland-Martin, who was elected as a member of the Jockey Club in June, 1975: 'He was a very straight foal. Always had tremendous character. He was a tough sort and even in the paddock at an early age he always wanted to be the boss among the other horses and they respected him for this. The only trouble with him, and it was obvious from the early days, was his colour. He has those easily recognizable blond streaks in his mane and tail and looked a little flashy. He was not a wishy-washy colt or a trigger type of flashy. The father of Word from Lundy, Worden II, was very simi-lar. I always thought that his colour would count against him whenever we sent him up to the sales. You can marry Einstein to an actress but to develop the perfect brain or the special body you have got to have the right upbringing.'

Grundy's constant companion in these early days was Overbury's stud groom Peter Diamond, who certainly gave him a special upbringing. He told me: 'I looked after him from the moment he came back from Ireland. He was a tough sort, never beaten in the paddock. He really was the cock of the walk, always the master. He was not going to be knocked about by anybody or anything. At that stage we bar break them and lunge them in. He was bitted and followed the routine of a racing stable, although nobody ever sat on his back until after he had gone to the sales. He would have an hour's exercise in the morning and the same routine in the afternoon. He was pretty lively with plenty of go in him. He would try and show off when we lunged him. He was never sick or sorry all the time he was with us. Some colts get slightly damaged when they bump into a rail. But he was perfect and was never off his grub for a day. He was a good doer. Actually he was a bit of a playboy and he used to spar with you when you went into his box. But there was no vice in him.

'I know it is easy to say afterwards but I always thought that he would win races. We knew that his colour was against him when we took him up to the sales. My father was a stud groom and he said: "Good hay and good oats and the horse will do the rest." That is what we have always done at Overbury and that's how it was with Grundy.'

Friday, October 5th, 1973 was the all-important day when this yearling was taken to the sales at Newmarket – to the very place where his great grand-dam had once changed hands for just thirty-five guineas. But this time it was to be a different story and one of racing's shrewdest judges had already visited Overbury to see the yearlings but was still by no means over keen to buy the son of Great Nephew, so unproven as a sire.

This was Keith Freeman, the Norwich-based bloodstock agent who finally did buy Grundy and manages the British racing affairs of the wealthy Milan industrialist Dr Carlo Vittadini.

The year of 1975 will be remembered for the way Italian-owned horses swept the board in England. We first saw Bolkonski take the 2,000 Guineas for owner C. D'Alessio, ridden by tiny Sardinian Franco Dettori. And as autumn leaves began to fall at Doncaster, Take Your Place won the *Observer* Gold Cup for the same owner. Dettori, who had a magnificent year with fourteen wins from only twenty rides, also won the Dewhurst Stakes on Wollow, who became justifiable winter favourite for the 2,000 Guineas. But in-between these Henry Cecil-trained triumphs it was the friendly, smiling figure of Carlo Vittadini who graced the winners' enclosures at Epsom, the Curragh and Ascot.

Vittadini had always been interested in horses in his native Italy. He loved hunting and his father was a keen hunt rider till he was over seventy years old. As an amateur rider he won thirty races on the Flat. His first ever horse was called Brush and he turned out to be a winner. It was a natural step that Vittadini should become interested in breeding. His stud farm was on the shores of Lake Maggiore, near

Dormello. It was at Dormello that the legendary Ribot was sired.

In 1956 Vittadini sent his trainer, Mario Benetti, to the last Tattersalls' sales at Doncaster. It was here that Carlo really got to know Keith Freeman.

Palatch was another successful horse for Vittadini in England winning the Yorkshire Oaks and Musidora. She was a difficult mare to train and Carlo was amused to find that her name meant 'Hangman' in Russian. She did nothing wrong at stud and was the mother of Voltiguer and Lingfield Derby Trial winner Patch. In his early days Vittadini raced his colts in Italy and his fillies in England. No Mercy is at the Upend Stud, having won the Free Handicap and Prix de Meautry. Among his first crop was the speedy Gentilhombre. In Italy his Accrale won the Gran Premio d'Italia and d'Milano and went on to sire his second winner of the Derby Italiano, Ardale, whose dam, Arandena, was also bought at Newmarket as a yearling.

But it was when Ortis, Habat and Grundy appeared on the scene that Vittadini became really well-known in England. After his exploits in 1975 – three Derby winners and a close-up second in the top Classics in England, Ireland, France and Italy, it was hardly surprising that he was voted Owner of the Year by the Horserace Writers' Association. He further cemented his association with England when buying the Beech House Stud at Newmarket from Louis Freedman at the end of the 1975 Flat season.

At the October sales in 1975 I met Freeman. Almost two years to the day that he bought Grundy we sat in his favourite position at the sales ring. He explained: 'I always sit just to the right of the auctioneer.' Bidding moved along smartly, the electrically operated number board indicating the number of the actual lot being sold. Freeman studied his catalogue carefully. Every lot had some notation against it. Sires and dams had been ringed by his knowledgeable pen. This was an expert about his work but he could easily have let Grundy slip from his grasp.

Friendly Freeman added: 'I have one absolute principle in the buying of yearlings and I stick to it rigidly. I never attempt to bid for any yearling whose mare has run at two miles. I am very fussy about that. But rules are made to be broken and with the Word from Lundy colt I made an exception. There were three things which I disliked about the colt. His sire Great Nephew never appealed to me for half a second, Word from Lundy ran over two miles and, of course, the other thing very much against Grundy was his colour. Yearlings from my own stud, the Bergh Apton Stud at Norwich, always go down to the Overbury Stud just before they go to the sales ring. I went to Overbury in September, 1973 and saw my own yearlings and all the others which were going to the sales. I am not being clever after the event but I fell in love with Grundy the moment I saw him being led round. It was love at first sight, but I remember saying to Tim Holland-Martin: "What a lovely colt – pity about his colour." Still, when he came up to the Houghton Sales Dr Vittadini and I had spoken about him and I had a note in my catalogue to bid up to 10000 guineas for him – not a penny more, as I was by no means keen to buy him.

'Funnily enough I was not sitting in my usual place when Grundy came into the ring. Dr Vittadini and myself were leaning over a rail away to the left of the auctioneer. I can't remember much about the early bidding but I know we thought we had got him at 9000 guineas. Then somebody else stepped in and we had to go to our maximum of 10000 guineas. Again somebody else stepped up the price and as it had gone over our limit both Dr Vittadini and I turned away. We had gone as far as we agreed. But he said: "Try one more." That is exactly what I did. I bid 11000 guineas and after a long silence he was finally knocked down to us for that price.'

Stud groom Peter Diamond recalls: 'I actually led Grundy round the sales ring that day and was pleased that we got such a good price. It was about what we expected. But when the auctioneer said: "Sold to Mr Keith Freeman," I was flabbergasted. When he saw the yearling at Overbury he was interested but repeatedly said that the colour put him off entirely. I was very shaken when I realized that Mr Freeman had in fact bought him. When you have five or six horses to lead round in the sales ring you get a bit dizzy and don't really take in all the bidding. I was sorry to part with Grundy that day. When you foal the yearlings and spend most of your time with them, feed them every morning and evening, you get to know them as characters. They become very much attached to you. I know Mr Freeman does not totally agree with our ideas of breeding lines at Overbury but he once told me: "Whatever I think, they all seem to win races." I felt sure that Grundy would turn into a racehorse and win races. But I hardly thought he would turn out to be what he was.' Diamond, who played a vital part in Grundy's early life, never saw Grundy again in the flesh until one never-to-be-forgotten day at Ascot – but that's another story.

Recalls Tim Holland-Martin, whose stud nestles amid Housman's 'coloured counties' at the foot of Bredon Hill,: 'I have since learnt that there were twenty-five under bidders for Grundy. But that always happens when you sell what turns out to be a great horse. People come up to you and say: "I really thought he was a good 'un and would love to have bid another couple of thousand guineas for him." Grundy did have a reserve on him but I don't think it was very high. I was certain his colour would put off Keith Freeman from buying. People are funny when they buy horses. I remember Vic Hardy, who had enjoyed great success with Tower Walk, telling Geoffrey Barling to buy him another horse. Geoffrey said: "We will have to pay a bit more now for the same sort." Hardy, who only owned two horses said: "If the next one costs twice as much he will have to be twice as good." Hardy was lucky as his second horse turned out to be Pat Eddery's first Derby ride, Pentland Firth.'

Having bought the Word from Lundy yearling the next job for Freeman was to find a suitable name. He told me: 'With all his buys Dr Vittadini sends me a list of possible names. I always like to take a part of the sire and mare when naming a horse. Dr Vittadini had several names lined up for him but after thinking about Great Nephew we finally agreed on Grundy. I had to write a letter to Dr Vittadini explaining the nursery rhyme about Grundy.'

Freeman's faith in Grundy – despite his colour – was yet another stroke of genius in a horse buying career which started way back in 1946. He said: 'Long periods of acute boredom in the Army did have one advantage. It gave me time to think what I would do when the war ended. I decided that I would spend my life dealing with horseracing and, in particular, the breeding side. I came out of the war with eighty pounds. I arranged with my local Lloyds Bank manager to raise an overdraft. He asked me if I had any security and when I replied "No" he was rather surprised. He asked me how much I needed to get going and I said: "£1000." He said kindly: "You had better have £1500," and that's how it all started and I have been with the same bank ever since. Over the years I must have bought hundreds of horses. Sometimes it can be up to 100 a year. I was lucky that I found a helpful bank manager. I have not made a fortune out of racing. I have simply shown a profit each year, refinancing my business from the sale of horses.

'I first came in contact with Carlo Vittadini in 1956. I was in Italy and was introduced to him, although at that stage he was little more than a face and a name. He had come into racing as an amateur jockey. He is a Dr because he has the Italian equivalent of an MA. Funnily enough his medicine firm in Milan is called ICI but, of course, it is not the same as the English-owned firm. Vittadini asked me to buy a yearling for him and at the last Doncaster sales in 1956 I bought a yearling called Exar for him for 1900 guineas. That's how our relationship started. He went to Italy and won simply everything, so I made a good start for a new client. Exar won the Gran Premio d'Milano and the Gran Premio d'Italia. Then in 1960 he was sent back to England and was trained at Newmarket by Noel Murless. That year he finished second in the Ascot Gold Cup but won the Goodwood and Doncaster cups, when ridden by Lester Piggott. This started Vittadini's interest in his own horses running in England. In 1971 his horse Ortis came to Newmarket. He was a strong, wilful horse and not at all suited to Newmarket. It is not the ideal place for this sort of four-year-old. I always think that Newmarket is miles and miles of bugger all. Ortis wanted a different scene. I thought that Lambourn with its twisting gallops and winding country lanes was the ideal place. At that stage I was certain that Peter Walwyn was the trainer of the future. I regarded him as brilliant in those days and he has got even better. I had no hesitation recommending Dr Vittadini to send Ortis to Peter. We ran him in the Hardwicke Stakes at Royal Ascot and he won by eight lengths. He really loved soft going.

'The next good horse I bought for Dr Vittadini was Habat. I went to Ireland and absolutely loved the grey Habitat colt. I recommended to Dr Vittadini that there was no limit for this one. I really loved the look of him. When the sales came round I admit that I kept bullying Dr Vittadini into buying him. When the bidding had soared up to 13000 guineas he turned to me and said: "Stop. There simply has got to be a limit to everything!" My good friend, the Marchioness of Tavistock, was sitting with Dr Vittadini and myself and she pressed me to have one more bid on his behalf. As I was sitting behind him I just gave another nod and got Habat for 14500 guineas. I don't think Dr Vittadini realized that the last bid was in fact on his behalf until they announced: "Sold to Mr Keith Freeman."

'In my lifetime I think there have been three outstanding jockeys – Lester Piggott, Pat Eddery and Enrico Camici, the Italian rider who partnered Ribot and Nearco. Pat's great strength is that he imparts a feeling of confidence to the horse. There is a current between rider and horse when Pat is in the saddle. Added to this is the priceless gift that he never loses his cool. Some people have a horse sense and Pat has it probably more than most. Some people can walk up to a horse without any problem. Others are certain to get kicked. Pat has a sympathy for the horses and they seem to sense this. After a race he can give you a clear insight into the running of your horse and also tell you how all the others have run in the same race. Grundy has been a relatively easy horse to ride. He just needed to see daylight and that was that. He had a genius in Peter Walwyn to train him. He seems to be able to teach horses manners as well as to run fast. Owner, trainer, jockey and racing manager form an intricate jig-saw and from all the opinions the plans are based. Actually I am sure the racing manager is the least important of the four. I always had two or three phone calls each week to Dr Vittadini and Peter Walwyn. I could spend an hour or more discussing the plans, alternative programmes and post-mortems. They are all very helpful. Dr Vittadini has been lucky in that eighty per cent of the horses I have bought for him have turned out to be winners. As a child of fifteen I once plucked up courage to ask the Aga Khan how he judged a yearling. Being so young I suppose I was bound to get an answer. He told me: "Train your eye to look at a horse as a whole. Instantly see the complete horse. If you don't like him in any minute detail, go away. If you see a damaging fault, work over the detail and see whether it is worth taking a chance." It is a method I have always tried to adopt. We were lucky in that Habat was top of the English Free Handicap one year and Grundy was the next.'

Freeman was actually the first man ever to bid 100000 guineas for a horse at the Park Paddocks, Newmarket. He broke the barrier for Vaguely Noble before he finally went for 136000 guineas on December 7th, 1967. The most he has ever paid for a yearling was 60000 guineas for Dumka, who subsequently won the French 1,000 Guineas for the Aga Khan. Yet he recalls: 'The first horse I ever bought cost nine guineas.' He has an interesting link with Lundy Parrot as he has not missed a single Newmarket sale since the war and must have looked on as Grundy's great grand-dam changed hands for thirty-five guineas. Says Keith: 'When they broke up the old sales ring at the Park Paddocks, which was a bit to the left of the existing one, I was keen to get the actual ring. I paid the foreman a fiver for it and it is now at my stud at Bergh Apton. So the ring where the unknown Lundy Parrot was once sold is now used at Freeman's stud in the lunging ring.

There is another interesting link between the Overbury stud, Keith Freeman and Grundy. As I have mentioned all of Freeman's yearlings spend a short time at Overbury prior to going to the various sales rings. Freeman bred a yearling by St Paddy called Patch and he enjoyed a short stay at

Overbury and actually shared the same paddock as the youthful Grundy. Says Tim Holland-Martin: 'We are rather proud that at one time we had the future English and Irish Derby winner Grundy in the very same paddock as Patch, who was only beaten a head in the Prix du Jockey Club at Chantilly, the French equivalent of the Derby.' Ironically Patch was to be bought by Carlo Vittadini and after a start to his career in Italy came to Lambourn and was housed in the same yard as Grundy with Peter Walwyn.

It was at Seven Barrows that Grundy came under the masterful eye of Peter Walwyn. Recalling Grundy's early days in the stables Walwyn says: 'He was basically a quiet character but he was no dead dog. Of course, one always rated him very highly but it was impossible at the very start to foresee how brilliant he was going to be.'

Bred by an out-and-out front-runner Walwyn could have been tempted to exploit Grundy's naturally brilliant speed. But he showed great patience and transformed the somewhat lively yearling into a fully matured Classic animal. Mention must also be made of Grundy's work-rider, Matt McCormack, who played a very vital role in the success story. As assistant head lad to Walwyn he helped to fashion Grundy into greatness. At one time Matt was with Noel Murless. During this period he rode such good horses as Mysterious, Lorenzaccio and Welsh Pageant. On the eve of the 1975 Derby Matt confided: 'I have never sat on a horse so perfectly tuned. Nor have I sat on one who has given me such a feel as he has done.' It was the skill of Walwyn and McCormack at home which enabled Grundy to be a more relaxed colt, able to settle in his races and giving him the chance to stay the $1\frac{1}{2}$ mile Derby trip. With less brilliant homework and loving tutors Grundy could well have been just another horse. Great Nephew was known for his liking to cut out the running. Brough Scott was in France during several of his big race wins and recalls: 'He simply pissed off with his rider and they never got a hold of him. Teaching Grundy to settle was probably the most important factor in his entire career. When he started on the gallops he was attempting to break the world speed record.'

Pat Eddery takes up the story of how the colt with the colouring nobody liked turned into a household name. He said: 'In his early two-year-old days I first saw Grundy in the yard. I ride out at Seven Barrows every Tuesday and Friday morning and can remember one of the lads commenting on Grundy but at that time I did not take much notice. Then one day I worked Grundy and I came back and told the guv'nor that I thought he was a lovely horse. It's hard to describe, but I had that special feel. We also had another good unraced two-year-old called No Alimony and I thought that he, too, was a pretty decent animal.

'When the final declarations were made for the Granville Stakes over six furlongs at Ascot on July 26th, 1974 the guv'-nor ran two – Grundy and No Alimony. I knew that these were two colts with more than normal ability. But I had the choice of rides and I went for Grundy. I would have staked my right arm that he would finish in front. Everybody knows now that Grundy won as he liked and it was No Alimony who followed us home, some two lengths behind.'

Grundy started at 5–1 for his first ever race. In his entire career he never started at odds as generous as this again – except when he won the Epsom Derby when his starting price was also 5–1. After his Ascot debut he was a 'hot-pot' and the bookmakers gave precious little away.

It is worth noting John Sharratt's astute reading of Grundy's first race in the *Raceform* note-book. His shrewd observation was: 'Grundy looked a cut above the average in the paddock and his running confirmed the impression. Going for a gap on the rails in the last furlong, he had to wriggle his way through but, once in front, soon put the issue beyond any doubt.'

Grundy's next race was the Sirenia Plate over six furlongs at Kempton on August 30th. Says Pat: 'He won in a hack canter but admittedly he did not have much to beat that day.' Hawk-eyed Sharratt noted: 'Grundy looked a picture in the paddock and his manner of racing left no doubt that he has the makings of a top-class colt. In front before halfway, he toyed with his field without ever being asked a question.' That day he started at 6–4 on and beat

Two shock defeats for the great Grundy in 1975 . . . beaten by Mark
Anthony (Lester Piggott) in the Greenham Stakes at Newbury and
(below) pipped by Bolkonski in the 2,000 Guineas at Newmarket.

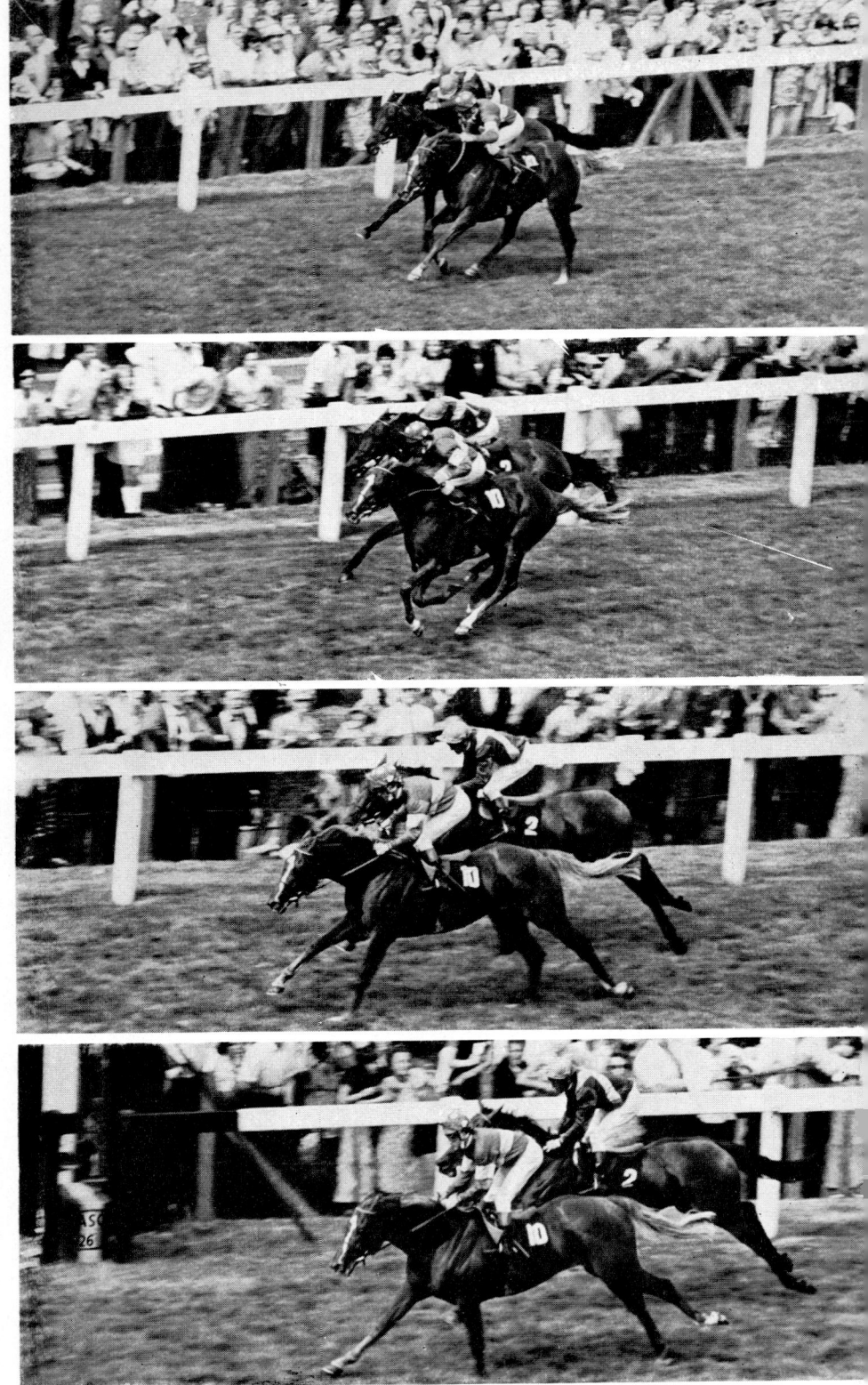

(Opposite) The greatest finish of all time as the great Grundy and Bustino fight out the fabulous ending to the 'King George VI' at Ascot, 1975.

(Right) Grundy and Eddery win the richest-ever Epsom Derby with the filly Nobiliary second.

(Below) Dr Carlo Vittadini, the Milan-based owner and his racing manager Keith Freeman (centre) greeting Grundy at The Curragh after the Irish Derby.

Grundy in full flight with Pat Eddery aboard. *(Below)* The record British money-winner is pictured with his regular work rider Matt McCormack just before his retirement was announced.

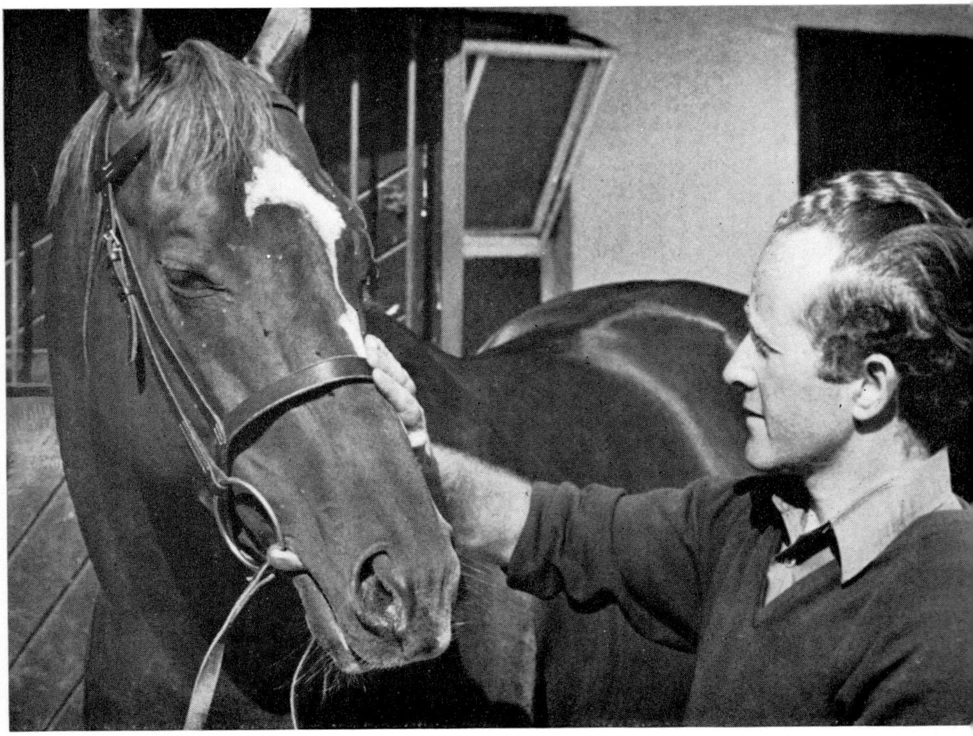

Prospect Rainbow by 2½ lengths. At this time I was on a cricket tour in Devon organized by Tony Fairbairn, Director General of the Racing Information Bureau. Our game that day was rained off and after a very liquid lunch, the entire team, called The Boffins, invaded a back street betting office in Ottery St Mary and backed Grundy to a man. We never had a moment's worry and we left the shop in high spirits leaving behind a bookie cursing the day the heavens opened and our match was cancelled.

Next stop for Grundy was the Champagne Stakes at Doncaster over seven furlongs on September 11th, when he beat Lester Piggott on Whip it Quick by half a length. He started 13–8 favourite and by now was being talked about as the best English-trained two-year-old, although the Irish jungle drums were beating out the name of Ravi Tikkoo's Steel Heart as a lively contender. Steel Heart duly won the Middle Park Stakes at Newmarket on October 3rd and it was clear that the Dewhurst Stakes was something of a match between Grundy and the Dermot Weld-trained raider.

Eddery wastes few words in describing his six lengths win over Steel Heart in the Dewhurst. He says simply: 'We pissed in.' Nobody who saw the runaway triumph will argue with him. *Raceform* were impressed and recorded: 'Grundy moved up smoothly to lead two furlongs from home and, kept right up to his work, drew clear away on the final climb. This was a performance of distinction and he retires for the season a worthy favourite for the 2,000 Guineas.'

Of all Grundy's four wins as a two-year-old the last one was the most impressive. Steel Heart cost Ravi Tikkoo a staggering 71 000 guineas but he was clearly well beaten by Grundy in the Dewhurst. Steel Heart beat Mark Anthony by a neck in one of his early races at Phoenix Park and also looked a high-class colt in the making when beating Auction Ring by 1½ lengths in the Gimcrack Stakes at York. By the end of Grundy's two-year-old career Vittadini, Freeman, Walwyn and Eddery knew they had a fascinating summer to look forward to. Says Freeman: 'After the Dewhurst Stakes I was talking to Fred Day, the top vet at Newmarket. He told me: "That was the most impressive Dewhurst Stakes winner I have ever seen. He gave away the sign of a really great horse. Not only did he quicken but he lengthened his stride. That's the vital thing." I saw a replay of the race in a film in the Stewards' room and was greatly impressed. Grundy gave the impression that he was top-class and could win at any distance from five furlongs to two miles. He was definitely staying on at the end of the Dewhurst. I am not a betting man and have only had a few wagers over the years but after the Dewhurst I contacted the bookmakers and had twenty pounds on Grundy for the following season's Triple Crown at 100–1.' Ironically Grundy was to be pipped in the first leg of the Triple Crown, win the second, and be a non-runner in the third. But the previous autumn just after the Dewhurst he looked a fine prospect. Still, racing is an odd game and Freeman rightly observes: 'You learn about this game until the day you die. Often you are made to realize the depth of your ignorance.'

March 17th was the next important day in the life of Grundy and the bad news which was announced by Peter Walwyn at Seven Barrows sent a shudder down the spine of all punters who had backed the colt ante-post for the Classics. Eddery says: 'I shall not forget the day in a hurry. I was riding Record Token from the stable yard through the covered ride. As the string of three-year-olds were making their way along, Corby kicked Grundy in the face. He did not bleed badly but it was clear that he had a terrible dent in his face, just under his left eye. Of course, it was a very worrying moment and while he did not bleed greatly there was the instant fear that he might have affected his breathing and the possibility of a sinus complaint.'

Keith Freeman was in South Africa at this time for their yearling sales. He says: 'I remember the phone ringing and Peter Walwyn coming on the end of the line. I said: "I don't mind what it is as long as it is not Grundy." Peter told me that it was and relayed the bad news to me. It was a shattering blow.'

Walwyn, with more than one possible 2,000 Guineas hope in Grundy, No Alimony, Consol and Corby had already planned the future races for his star juveniles. The initial plan was to run Grundy in the 2,000 Guineas Trial at Ascot on April 12th. But because of the setback in Grundy's work it was decided that his re-appearance should be put back a week for the Greenham Stakes at Newbury on April 19th. Says Pat: 'A speck of blood did come out of Grundy's nose when he came back to work. But I think that he was just cleaning himself out.' Walwyn said: 'After he was kicked he stayed in his box for one day, was taken out walking for the next two and then trotted again. He was back cantering in a week.' Having disregarded plans to run Grundy in the Ascot race he was later tempted to run Grundy in the slightly easier Classic Trial at Thirsk on the same day as the Greenham. Over the years the Greenham has proved a real grave-yard for Classic hopefuls. Peter Walwyn's Lunchtime started at 11-4 on for the race only to be beaten and several other top-class colts were beaten in this re-appearance race. In fact the last horse to win the Greenham and then go on to take the 2,000 Guineas was Orwell, way back in 1932. High Top did land the Thirsk Classic Trial–2,000 Guineas double in 1972. Before making the decision to run Grundy at Newbury Walwyn admitted: 'I hate the Greenham in every way. It always seems to produce such horrible results. Even when Mill Reef won there he went on to be beaten in the 2,000 Guineas. I know that Newbury is a very fair course over seven furlongs and the timing of the race is good, just four-teen days before the Guineas. Circumstances may force me to run Grundy at Newbury but I loathe the race.' Grundy's injury, a really vicious kick from Corby, came at the very worst time in his preparation and I refuse to believe that he would ever have been beaten in the Greenham but for the setback. In the same way one can say that Nijinsky's routine was put out by a slight attack of ringworm just before his St Leger win and he was slightly rushed in his work. When he was just touched off in the Arc de Triomphe the vital two or three days' work missed on the gallops probably made all the difference.

All Walwyn's fears about the Greenham came true with stark reality. Grundy, starting at 6-4 on, was beaten by two lengths by Mark Anthony, who had joined Clive Brittain's

Newmarket yard, having been purchased the previous autumn by Captain Marcos Lemos. Pat says: 'I gave Grundy the easiest race I possibly could, bearing in mind his accident. I bounced out well and was keen to get Grundy covered up as he always relaxed far better this way. If he saw too much daylight early on he was inclined to pull strongly and would not quieten down to do his best work. Unfortunately all the other jockeys were watching to see what I was up to and were pulling like mad, so I had to go on about $2\frac{1}{2}$ furlongs from home, which was not my ideal plan at all. It was pretty heavy going and in the final furlong I could not really find any extra. Lester Piggott on Mark Anthony was on my arse coming into the final furlong and just went storming past. I swore after the race that there would never be another time when Mark Anthony could possibly beat Grundy again – no way. I still maintain that Grundy was beaten that day by the loss of work and heavy going. I was really sick that Grundy had been beaten for the first time but was far from unhappy about his future.

'As I had really bolted in on No Alimony previously in the Craven Stakes, when we trounced Bolkonski by four lengths, people kept asking me which of our two colts I would ride in the 2,000 Guineas. Even after Grundy's defeat in the Greenham I was certain that he was the better of the two. People kept telling me that I had picked the wrong one. But I knew that I had made the right decision when Grundy and No Alimony had their first ever race and I was certain that I had gone for the right one again.'

The 1975 Guineas meeting will be remembered for the Battle of Newmarket and the antics of the striking stable lads. Eddery duly picked Grundy for the 2,000 Guineas while Frank Morby, a much underrated rider, partnered No Alimony. Morby waited until he was forty for his first Classic ride. At one stage of his career he went eight years without riding a winner. But by riding out for as many as eight trainers in one week he started to pick up spare rides. Previously he worked as stable lad to the late Bernard van Cutsem at Newmarket. After a lack-lustre apprenticeship he seemed to have little future in racing. But this cheerful character has bounced back to the top and was highly rated by Peter Walwyn as not only a reliable second jockey but also a fine work rider, able to judge when horses are at their peak. Says Morby: 'For about a dozen years I rode hairy, scary rough and mad horses that no one else would ride and I have got the scars to prove it. I've broken twenty bones in my body and that is why with Peter Walwyn and Fulke Johnson Houghton behind me I am now able to turn those sort of rides down. But at one time I simply had to accept those nightmare rides just to make a living.'

Grundy started at 7–2 favourite but for the only time in his life lost his second successive race. Recalls Pat: 'Here again I think we were bloody unlucky. The stable lads were making a hell of a noise and there was a lot of shouting going on. I agreed with the lads that they deserved more money. Good luck to them, I thought. I expected them to make some kind of a demonstration but I did think that they would allow the 2,000 Guineas to be run without any trouble. Perhaps the lads knew that I was on their side to a certain extent because as I went down to the start they never gave me any trouble. They were bloody awful to some of the other jockeys. When Grundy and I got down to the start we were fairly quickly put into the stalls. But with all the bother going on we were stuck in there for about five minutes. Poor Grundy had never seen anything like this in his life and did not know what was going on. Naturally he got very excited. Then we were let out of the stalls and brought round in front of them for a flag start. We started quite a way in front of the stalls so the distance of the race was not strictly accurate. I had ridden Grundy at work twice that week and I was certain that he was a far better horse for the 2,000 Guineas than the Greenham. But the lads played up like hell and it did make a difference. Not going a full mile was also important. I led about $2\frac{1}{2}$ furlongs out and thought that I was okay. Then Bolkonski appeared on the scene. But even then Grundy came back at him towards the end and we only lost by half a length. In a few more strides we would have won. But the great thing was that he was staying on at the finish and I knew then that he would get the trip in the Derby without any trouble.'

After Grundy had been beaten in the Greenham, Walwyn said: 'I never make excuses for any beaten horses, but make no mistake, Grundy will never lose to Mark Anthony again.' This proved to be the case as Mark Anthony and Lester Piggott finished sixth, some five lengths behind Grundy. No Alimony finished fifteenth to vindicate Eddery's wise choice of mounts. Having seen Grundy lose two successive races Walwyn and Eddery could not have been blamed if they lost a little faith in their star. But they did not budge an inch in their opinion that he was a really top-class colt, even though, like his sire Great Nephew, he had finished second in the 2,000 Guineas.

The day after Grundy's Guineas defeat I telephoned Walwyn to obtain his views. 'With all those lunatics running around over Newmarket heath he was bound to be upset. We will now go for the Irish Guineas,' was Walwyn's announcement. He did have a slight doubt at this stage about the Derby and admitted: 'If he wins the Irish Guineas going away we will have to think very seriously about Epsom. I am pretty sure that he will stay a mile and a quarter but there is a doubt about the last two furlongs.'

The Walwyn-Eddery trip to Ireland for the Guineas meeting was somewhat hectic. As they waited on the runway at Heathrow on the Friday – the 1,000 Guineas was run that evening – they were unlucky enough to be rammed by another plane. Or in the more graphic words of Pat: 'A jumbo jet hit us up the arse.' A lengthy delay caused grave concern and by the time the Grundy party had arrived at Dublin airport time was getting very much against them and the ride for Pat on Silky in the 1,000 Guineas was beginning to look a forlorn hope. But enterprising pressman Jonathan Powell of the *Sunday People*, who was on the same flight, had a hired car awaiting his delayed arrival and with some highly illegal manoeuvres through rush-hour Dublin traffic deposited the hero at the course just in time to weigh out for Silky. Sadly there was no fairy-tale ending for Pat as he finished second on Silky, a daughter of Nijinsky, to Miralle, who was ridden by that ex-cockney turned Irish jockey Buster Parnell. This likable character's claim to fame is that he will never say one word when he can find a kindly ear who will listen to about ten thousand. He could out-talk Muhammad Ali and Richard Pitman without so much as a sip of water. Still, it was not all disappointments that evening for Eddery. He did win on Consol and went on to complete a double on the Willie Robinson-trained Starduster. From three rides at the Curragh he had two wins and a second – a far cry from the kid who once finished a tailed-off last in his first ever race on the same course some six years previously.

Says Eddery: 'Christ, he was getting a better horse every time I sat on him. I was sure that he would win the Irish Guineas after his last work with me at Lambourn. I really fancied him a hell of a lot.' Jonathan Powell has shown me his fascinating video films of Grundy's triumphs over and over again. The way Grundy cantered away with the Irish Guineas was a first-class performance and, in hindsight, those of us who sided with the French-trained Green Dancer for the Epsom Derby should have made a speedy trip to the nearest optician. The replay shows that Grundy, looking magnificent in the paddock, was second in the early stages of the race at the Curragh on May 17th. Carlo Vittadini's blue colours with the yellow hoop were first seen in front some two furlongs out when Grundy swept through to challenge. In a few strides it was all over, although Piggott on Mark Anthony did look menacing at one stage, only to finish third. Grundy had 1½ lengths to spare over the French trained Monsanto at the line.

After this victory – Grundy's first as a three-year-old – it was obvious that he would have to be in the Epsom line-up. Here again Walwyn held several aces in his hand. But Corby was soon shuffled from the Derby pack when he was beaten by Hobnob in York's Dante Stakes. Another possible Derby ride for Eddery emerged – or rather flew – onto the scene when Patch ran in the Derby Trial at Lingfield. Back from Italy he joined Walwyn and ran in the same colours as Grundy. In Italy he had finished third in the Gran Criterium in Milan the previous October but had been a close-up second in the Premio Vittorio Crespi, also in Milan. Clearly he was suited by long distances. But it was the long distance by which he won at Lingfield which stamped him out as a colt of top-class potential. He made all with Eddery on board and won unchallenged by ten lengths from Anne's Pretender. Romper, at that time the only Derby contender with an actual win at Epsom, and the much talked about Noel Murless colt Bold Aussie were beaten out of sight in this shock procession. The fact that Patch drifted from 6–1 to 10–1 in the market showed what a surprise his triumph was.

By late May the Derby picture was becoming much clearer Walwyn led a triple challenge with Grundy (Pat Eddery), No Alimony (Joe Mercer) and Red Regent (Brian Taylor). Sportingly he released Frank Morby so that he could partner Romper.

The previous year's *Observer* Gold Cup was, perhaps, the best clue as to what would happen in the Derby. Alec Head sent over Green Dancer to win by 1½ lengths from Sea Break with No Alimony ¾ of a length away third. Eddery was convinced that Grundy would have won the *Observer*. He always rated him better than No Alimony and on this basis was delighted when he finished so close behind Green Dancer and Sea Break. Then another race finally convinced Pat that whenever Green Dancer and Grundy clashed head-on he would be on the winner. Green Dancer was a son of the great Nijinsky and was clearly an exceptional colt. The English pressman who went over for the Poule d'Essai des Poulains at Longchamp on April 27th were all convinced that they had seen the genuine Derby favourite, if not the winner. Freddie Head has few equals round the Paris circuit and he was seen at his best that day when winning by a length. But it was the horse who finished sixth who made Eddery more and more certain that he would win the Derby. He says: 'I was sixth on Record Token that day and saw Green Dancer go flying by. Sure he was impressive. But Record Token was a class below Grundy and I was sure that Grundy would have beaten Green Dancer that day – gobbled him up. Record Token was not a class below Grundy, he was two classes. But finishing well on him made me think that Green Dancer was not all he was cracked up to be. I had finished nearer to him on No Alimony and Record Token but Grundy had two higher gears than those two. Because of all this I thought I had a great chance in the Derby. Grundy stayed on in the English 2,000 Guineas and pissed up in Ireland. I honestly couldn't see him being beaten at Epsom.'

If Green Dancer was impressive in his first race of the season at Longchamp he was even more so on May 18th when he waltzed away with the Prix Lupin. There was a great deal to like about the way he got his head in front and battled on gamely to defeat Mariacci by $\frac{3}{4}$ of a length. This was real pre-Derby form. Perhaps those of us who saw Green Dancer as the biggest Derby certainty for a long time – possibly since his father won in 1970 – should have remembered Alec Head's unfortunate record at Epsom. He won the 1956 Derby with Levandin but since then his efforts have been haunted by cruel luck and misfortune. Bourbon became so excited before the race that he neatly deposited Freddie Head on his backside in the parade and there was worse to follow. Lyphard was seen as a 'real good thing' on form but Head Jnr decided to take him on the widest possible route round Tattenham Corner and some irate punters were unkind enough to ask whether in fact he was trying to steer the French raider in the direction of Ewell High Street. But all that was forgotten when Green Dancer arrived at Epsom. Surely Head's hoodoo would be smashed by this silken speedster. There was only one fear concerning Green Dancer, a niggling feeling which was to become an expensive reality at Epsom. In his last race at Longchamp, prior to the Derby, he was impressive. But there was the slightest hint that perhaps he was not truly going to get the testing $1\frac{1}{2}$ miles at Epsom. In hindsight this was probably his downfall and Alec Head seldom raced him over the Derby distance later in his career. Freddie Head was on his honeymoon when he rode Green Dancer, the 6–4 favourite, in the Derby. But there was to be no fairy-tale ending and this seemingly powerful duo were relegated to sixth.

To say Eddery rode a perfect race on Grundy in the Derby on June 4th is an understatement. He rode the 5–1 chance with a coolness well in advance of his young years. He handled Grundy as though he had no stamina doubts whatsoever and at every stage of the race was perfectly placed in the leading group. The video recording of the memorable race shows that Eddery's dash and judgement combined to send Grundy home a relatively easy three lengths winner. It was Ryan Price's third-string Carolus who made the early running with Tanzor last. Like Green Dancer, a son of Nijinsky, Tanzor was always stone cold last and never gave a second of fear for those punters who had taken the attractive odds of 5–1 against him finishing last. Looking back on the 1975 season this was the biggest certainty of them all. It was almost like stealing money from the bookmakers. He was still struggling down the straight when Pat was on the scales.

It was coming round Tattenham Corner where Eddery's genius was best spotted. He was fourth on Grundy into the straight having gone on the inside of Carolus and Nuthatch and then switched with minimum change of action to speed past stable-companion Red Regent on his outside. Zooming into the straight it was Anne's Pretender who sprinted for home. He and Tony Murray built up quite a lead. It was the kind of lead the 50–1 outsider Snow Knight had stolen the year before and gone on to win. But there was to be no similar long-priced runaway hero this time. Turning into the straight Eddery was still some five lengths behind Tony Murray on Anne's Pretender. Two furlongs out he had cruised into second place but was still two lengths adrift. It was then that Grundy's brilliance took the honours. Eddery used his whip eight times and this magnificent colt with the flowing flaxen mane and tail responded superbly. Watching countless replays of this race gives you the chance to spot several interesting factors. Hobnob went wide at Tattenham Corner and took out the grey Bruni with Lester Piggott on board. But for this I think Bruni would have finished much closer than his final fourteenth position and his subsequent runaway win in the St Leger would not have been such a shock. Green Dancer did make some progress in the straight but was never in a position to challenge. Anne's Pretender eventually finished fourth and second place went to the only filly in the race, Nobiliary. Her trainer Maurice Zilber rated her so highly that he refused to let her run in the Oaks and was quite happy to let his filly take on the colts. Zilber, a remarkable man who made his fortune as a gambler on the racetracks of Paris, was proved correct and but for Grundy the filly would have produced the turn-up of the century, and also struck a huge blow for Women's Lib. Zilber, incidentally, had previously declared 'Grundy – he no stay', but that proved to be quite incorrect. Frankie Durr, good as ever at the ripe old age of forty-eight, finished third on Hunza Dancer, who had only Tanzor behind him turning into the straight and went past everything on the far rail like an express train to finish third. *Raceform* expert John Sharratt noted: 'Grundy, cool and collected in the preliminaries, proved himself without doubt the best horse on the day. Tucked in behind the leading trio he was asked for his effort below the distance and from that moment the result was never in question.' Of the ill-fated Green Dancer Sharratt observed: 'He looked terribly lean and fine drawn and his running reflected his appearance.'

At the end of Grundy's career Eddery and I had a lengthy conversation about his favourite horse. He told me: 'Of course after winning the King George I felt a million dollars. But winning the Epsom Derby was *the* race. It's the one which I will always cherish more than any other race. Let's face it, there's only one English Derby and Grundy proved beyond doubt that he was the best three-year-old in the business. Everything went like a dream for me in the race and when I went for the gaps nothing went wrong or got in my way. I was certain after the Irish Guineas that he would stay and I always said we were a certainty to win the Derby. Coming round Tattenham Corner I had no worries because I was so close to the first group. One furlong out I thought to myself: "God, you have a great chance. This is really it." But I kept saying to myself: "Go on old boy, go on old boy." Having seen so many re-runs of films of previous Derbys I was certain that something would come and do for us before the winning-post. I was just waiting for the terrible moment but it never came. Christ, it was some relief I can tell you. I just eased him up on the line and gave him a pat as we went past the winning-post. Grundy gave me some wonderful memories but I will always think of him that day at Epsom and remember that the English Derby was my race.'

After the race John Rickman interviewed Pat Eddery. 'You had to hit him?' inquired the famous hat-raiser. Eddery, looking somewhat confused by the dialogue, replied simply 'Yes' and gave one of his boyish grins. In the winners' enclosure it was Peter Walwyn, a big man in every sense of the word, who stole the show. Carlo Vittadini and Keith Freeman were soon at the horse's head giving him loving pats. But it was Walwyn, who removed his top hat in the winners' enclosure as if in the presence of greatness, who looked the most pleased. 'What are you going to do with him now?' asked one of the pressmen involved in the annual rugby scrum for quotes in the winners' enclosure. 'I don't know what he is going to do but I know what I am going to do,' replied Walwyn with the obvious joy of a man who had trained a horse to perfection to win this elusive race and with it the important £106 000 prize-money. At moments like these the money aspect is pushed to one side. The glory of winning the race is enough. Walwyn and his party duly moved on to the nearest bar and I don't suppose the gulps of champagne have ever tasted sweeter. Pat Eddery was whisked away to the Royal Box. He says: 'The Queen was terribly excited about Grundy's win and we talked for a long time about the race. She was very nice and from the conversation I immediately realized that she knew a lot about racing. Having won the race I was relieved that it was all over. That night Terry drove me home as usual. We had a nice dinner and I was in bed well before midnight. When I woke up the next morning it was wonderful. I suddenly thought: "Christ, I won the bloody Derby yesterday." '

Grundy's winning time for the Derby was 2 minutes, 35.5 seconds. 'I rode him on a long rein and he just lobbed along for the first mile,' Pat recounted later. 'Everything went just perfectly.' Walwyn often spoke of Grundy as a 'tiger' and he certainly showed courage in coming back to win the Derby, when you recall that on March 17th he suffered a kick in the face just three inches below his left eye. The form of the

156

previous year's *Observer* Gold Cup went for the proverbial 'burton' as Green Dancer was a flop and the runner-up, Sea Break, finished thirteenth and No Alimony, third at Doncaster, was fifteenth. Sea Break, a highly temperamental horse, was disturbed by the exacting Derby preliminaries.

Next stop for Grundy was the Irish Derby at the Curragh on June 28th. A year before, Eddery lost the ride on the winner English Prince because of the Royal Ascot ban. But this time he was in charge of Grundy, who went to the Curragh as one of the hottest favourites ever in the race – a race, I may say, which has over the years seen some peculiar results. The defeat of Sir Ivor was just one of several turnabouts in the Epsom-Curragh Derby form. Eddery was certain that Grundy would win and before leaving for Ireland told me: 'He is a great horse and I promise you that he will win. People who backed him at Epsom must not desert him now. Some of the horses we beat at Epsom have run since and let the form down. Every year they try and find one to beat the Epsom winner in Ireland but I can't see it happening this time for one second.'

It was the subsequent Ascot defeat of Hunza Dancer which led many people to believe that the Derby form had not worked out well. Then Whip It Quick was also beaten at Ascot and those looking for an excuse to put something up against Grundy had these bits of ammunition. Before going over to Ireland Peter Walwyn said: 'The only weather to worry me would be rain. If the ground became terribly soft I would not dream of running Grundy. *Timeform* said in 1974 that he was a very good horse on the soft but he is nowhere as good in those conditions as he is on the firm.' Keeping a Classic colt at his best throughout the summer months is a very skilful art. It must be said that Walwyn did a magnificent job and when Grundy stepped into the parade ring at the Curragh he could not have looked better. After Grundy had won the Epsom Derby his *Timeform* rating was 142 – two more than the 1965 winner, Sea Bird II, and just one less than Sir Ivor (1968). At this stage little Mill Reef had been awarded 137, as had Roberto. So Grundy went to the Curragh with a terrific reputation behind him. When the race was over Grundy's reputation had soared to even dizzier heights. Peter O'Sullevan, comentating on the £64036 race from the Curragh, gave his usual faultless account of the running. In the early stages it was Yves Saint-Martin who led on Maitland. There was no great pace early on and with one mile to go Eddery had Grundy tucked in nicely in eighth position. At this point the race split into two groups with Grundy in front of the second party. Three furlongs out the pace quickened and with Grundy still some way behind the leading group Peter O'Sullevan observed: 'Grundy has got it to do.' But no sooner had he uttered these words than he was reporting: 'It's Grundy now streaking into the lead. It's Grundy winning like a real champion.' Grundy in fact had two lengths to spare over King Pellinore at the post with Anne's Pretender six lengths away third. The great Grundy had really shown his rivals the way home in the closing stages. Three and a half furlongs out Eddery was eighth on Grundy. But once he pulled out Grundy for a run it was all over. He gave Grundy one whack and riding out with hands and heels completed the Epsom-Curragh double, which has eluded many horses before him.

Having landed odds of 10–9 on to win the Irish Derby, Ladbrokes made him 6–4 on for the King George VI and Queen Elizabeth Diamond Stakes on July 26th. He was 5–4 on with William Hill. Just like at Epsom, Anne's Pretender had made a dash for the finish ahead of the pack but it was Grundy who sailed past him. At Epsom Grundy slowly but surely wore down Anne's Pretender. But in Ireland he was well back one second and then flying ahead the next. A three length deficit was translated into a going-away lead half a furlong from home. Grundy repeated the achievements of Santa Claus, who took the Irish 2,000 Guineas, Epsom Derby and then the Irish Sweeps Derby in 1964. The winning time was 2 minutes, 31.1 seconds – only two seconds outside the course record set up by Tambourine II in the inaugural Sweeps Derby in 1962. Says Pat, naturally delighted to win on his 'home' track: 'I was never going to lose at any stage. I was always going really easily and if the

Curragh is a harder test of stamina, Grundy never noticed it. I was just behind King Pellinore coming down the hill and I just moved up on the outside to take my position in the straight. It was a very easy win.' *Raceform*'s Irish representative agreed and recorded: 'Grundy, looking extremely well, was very cool in the preliminaries. Close up in seventh place on the final turn, he began a run two and a half furlongs down and, switched for a clear passage, hit the front below the distance. He could have won by double the winning margin if he had been ridden out.' Eddery again showed his liking for the Curragh by also winning the first day of the card, The Midsummer Scurry Handicap, on the Willie Robinson-trained Bold Tack.

The stage was now set for the King George VI and Queen Elizabeth Diamond Stakes at Ascot. At the first forfeit stage there were thirty-eight acceptors from six countries for the first prize of £81 910. Many Classic horses were among the acceptors and the great French mare Allez France was at one stage a likely runner. But the Wildenstein camp again decided against sending her over, which was a great shame. But with Dahlia, twice successful in the King George, and Dibidale, the 1974 Irish Guinness Oaks winner, in the field there was no lack of super stars. Also in the line-up was Lady Beaverbrook's Bustino, who won the previous season's St Leger. I spoke to Sir Gordon Richards – England's shortest knight – earlier in the week prior to the King George. He had just returned from West Ilsley after watching Bustino having his final pre-race gallop with Joe Mercer in the saddle. He told me: 'Major Dick Hern and I were very impressed. People are saying that he is an out and out stayer, who just plugs away. Because he won the St Leger people believe that he is purely a stayer. But that's a lot of cock. He is a very consistent and good horse. To say that he just plods along does not make sense when he has beaten the course record over the 1½ mile Derby trip at Epsom in the Coronation Cup and won the Lingfield Derby Trial in a fast time. He may be the staying sort, but he still has a remarkably good turn of foot.' Sir Gordon, who won the King George on Pinza in 1953 after their Derby triumph, added: 'Grundy was a damn good Derby winner – make no mistake of that. But Bustino has never run a bad race in his life and it will be a fascinating battle.' What made Bustino's Coronation Cup win so remarkable was that it was the first outing since he won the St Leger the previous season. It was a brilliant training performance by Dick Hern.

Early in the week millionaire art dealer and racing tycoon Daniel Wildenstein announced that Allez France would be a non-runner. For over thirty years Wildenstein has had something of a hoodoo when his horses have run in England. Allez France was beaten in the Champion Stakes in 1973 and this convinced him that he was never going to enjoy good fortune this side of the channel. But when Lianga won at Newmarket in 1975 it broke his duck and it was hoped that the wonder mare of Paris would be seen at Ascot. But after all the usual announcements and counter statements it was finally confirmed that Allez France, the Queen of Europe after her Arc win in 1974, would not take on Grundy and Bustino. But Wildenstein was represented by Ashmore. His reason for taking out Allez France was: 'She has traces of an allergy similar to hay fever. It will disappear when the hay is cut.' Maurice Zilber, undeterred by his previous incorrect judgement of Grundy, was again claiming before the King George: 'Grundy – he no stay at Ascot.' The Egyptian-born trainer seemed to have a 'thing' about Grundy not staying but he was to be proved incorrect yet again. York was to be Zilber's moment of triumph – except for the fact that he was not there to watch it.

I visited Seven Barrows on the Monday prior to the King George VI. Grundy's usual work-rider, Matt McCormack, gave him a brisk workout, watched with great interest by Walwyn. When Grundy posed for photographers after his work he seemed terribly bored by the whole affair. 'I think he's gone to sleep,' suggested Walwyn, clearly tense before such a vital race. His assistant trainer Jeremy Speid-Soote confided: 'You know the guv'nor. He's a bit on edge before such a big race. It's a tremendous responsibility.' Speid-Soote was, of course, a one-time jump jockey with Ryan Price and then started training himself. 'But I am far better off working for Peter,' he told me. 'I was having a hell of a job getting owners.'

Grundy's sale for one million pounds, with the Levy Board acquiring a three-quarter share, made the pressures even greater. After his win in the Irish Derby his value must have soared way past the two and a half million pounds mark. As we strolled through to his indoor gallop Walwyn commented: 'At one million pounds he could still turn out to be a cheap horse.' His handler defended the decision not to let Grundy race as a four-year-old. He told me: 'He's done enough already.' But the most memorable of Grundy's great triumphs was still around the corner. In the twenty-fifth running of the King George VI he was attempting to become the highest English-trained money winner ever in Europe. Victory at Ascot took his winnings to £312122. Mill Reef held the previous record with £300192. I think that people who praised Grundy were inclined at times to forget the part Eddery had played in his success. His riding of the chestnut speedster was faultless. Yet when he rode Grundy in Ascot's all-aged Classic he had only ever one previous run in the race. In 1973 he had partnered Park Lawn and had finished stone cold last of the twelve runners. Peter Walwyn had only two previous runners in the race and they had both finished second. A surprise French runner in the race was the Noel Pelat-trained On My Way, who was ridden by colourful Australian jockey Bill Pyers. The ginger-haired character won the race at his first attempt on Nasram II in 1964 and later went on to win with Dahlia. On My Way was a popular outsider and was backed down from 33-1 to 12-1, although he drifted out to 20-1 on the day of the race. In the previous twenty-four years the winners' score was England twelve, France seven, Ireland four and Italy one. Peter Walwyn's second jockey, Frank Morby, part-nered Libra's Rib, whose great sire Ribot won the 1956 King George on his only venture on English soil.

Besides Bustino, Lady Beaverbrook ran Highest and Kinglet as pacemakers. They certainly did their job well and the pace was a blistering one from the word go. But, ironi-cally, when the stalls flashed open it was Grundy and Bustino who came out first. A mile and a half later they were still locked in a desperate battle. Predictably the pacemakers took it up from the break and at the one mile marker it was obvious that this was going to be a very fast run race. Frankie Durr cut out the early pace on Highest for four and a half furlongs. Then it was Kinglet who led the star-studded field a mile from home. Highest, in fact, came to a near halt like a shot rabbit. Over half a mile from home and before the final turn before the straight, Joe Mercer swept Bustino to the front. Joe was to ride the race of his life on the very course where his brother Manny was so tragically killed. Just before the final turn Bustino was leading and Grundy was fourth. For one split second it seemed as though the dual Derby winner was not going to be able to match the leader's blistering pace. He was three lengths adrift and could easily have surrendered, but on entering the straight it was obvious that this thriller had developed into a titanic battle between Bustino and Grundy – the kind of ding-dong battle boxing promoters dream of. One furlong from home Grundy ranged upsides Bustino and that is when the struggle really developed. Grundy went on, having received twelve whacks from Eddery and three firm reminders before the two furlong marker. But Bustino would simply not give in and as he inched his way back the two were locked in this sensational finish. On the line Grundy had gained a half length advantage after a display of guts and courage few horses will ever offer. Just before the line Peter O'Sullevan told his millions of viewers: 'Bustino is fighting back . . . but Grundy is holding him.' I have heard the famous Hampden Park roar and heard the reception the Foster-slurping spectators on the Sydney Hill always extend to their hero, Doug Walters. But the noise at Ascot when Grundy and Bustino came to the finishing post was unbelievable. And above all the excitement the voice of Peter Walwyn could be heard screaming: 'Come on my son.' After the race was over Walwyn was virtually speechless and Eddery on dismounting could only say: 'What a great horse.' Grundy's performance put him on a level with Royal Palace (1967) and Crepello (1957) as the best home-bred Derby winners in recent years. Like Nijinsky he showed how a good three-year-old can slaughter his older rivals in the King George VI. Nijinsky beat the previous year's Derby winner Blakeney when he won the race.

Seconds after Grundy and Bustino had gone past the post it was revealed that both horses had beaten the Ascot course record. Grundy's winning time of 2 minutes, 26.98 seconds was a staggering 2.36 seconds faster than the $1\frac{1}{2}$ mile record. Walwyn told pressmen: 'I knew it had to be a record after such a finish.' When pressed about Grundy's future races he answered: 'To hell with the future. What has happened today is marvellous enough for anybody.' Almost unnoticed was Dahlia, who trailed in five lengths away third but even she smashed all previous timings for the race. Fourth was Pyers on On My Way while Card King, once bought out of a seller, was fifth. So far back as the winner and second were on their way to the ear-splitting reception were the pace-makers Kinglet and Highest. They had done their job in setting a lightning pace but the plan failed to work for the Beaverbrook brigade and Bustino had to take second place. Said Joe Mercer, who had sworn blind before the race that there was not a single three-year-old in Europe who could match Bustino: 'Grundy must be a great horse. Really great to have pipped us today.' Zilber had pronounced before the race: 'Dahlia – she ees back to 'er best, maka no mistake,' but the mare was completely forced out of the limelight by Grundy and Bustino. And for one man who had not seen Grundy since he was led round in the yearling sales ring it was an especially emotional moment.

Peter Diamond, Grundy's stud groom, had watched all his races on television but had not actually seen him in the flesh since he was bought by Keith Freeman at Newmarket. It was Diamond who had actually led Grundy round that day and was surprised that Freeman had bought him because of his colour. Said Peter: 'I had enjoyed watching his races on the telly but when the King George VI came up Mr Holland-Martin suggested that I should go along and have a look. I never had a single penny on Grundy all the time he ran. I am a little superstitious and I thought that if I had a plunge on him I might be a jinx and stop him winning. I was just pleased to see him win his races. I stood at the back of the stands at Ascot and watched the race. As they came round the final turn and the finish developed between Grundy and Bustino I simply could not bear to watch it. I was shaking like a leaf and had to turn away to the corner and walk out to a balcony where I could look down on the winners' enclosure. My heart was pumping and the excitement of it all was just too much. When Grundy came back and Pat Eddery steered him into the winners' enclosure I was near to tears. I could not believe that the yearling I had looked after had won this big race. You could work a lifetime as a stud groom and not have a horse like this ever again. There were so many people milling round Grundy after the race that I never really had a chance to get close to him. Some mares have left us and then come back. I'll swear that they know you again. They recognize the voice more than anything, I think. If you have been kind they recognize that as well. Horses remember kindness more than anything else. Still I never got close enough to Grundy to see whether he would remember me.' Tim Holland-Martin was another vital link in the Grundy success story who was worried about backing him. He said: 'I did not back him as a two-year-old, although I think I saw all his races. I did, however, take a chance and back him in a 2,000 Guineas–Derby double. It was when I saw the injury he had received and the hell of a hole on his head that I realized the full extent of the accident.'

Only one person will ever know the way Grundy felt throughout that epic battle and he is Pat Eddery. After a few months had gone by the young Irishman still saw the race clearly in his mind's eye He told me: 'I was determined to be near to Joe Mercer on Bustino throughout the race. But those two pacemakers meant that we were going like hell all the way. I have never known a pace like it for a race of that length. When Joe kicked on going towards the final turn I was about a length behind him and right on his arse, just as I wanted to be. But Bustino was a nippy little horse and he fairly scooted round the bend. Grundy, although he acted at Epsom perfectly, did not, for some reason, take that corner at Ascot so well. He was a big long striding horse and his action did not allow him to go round that corner nearly as well as Bustino. I suppose he must have stolen four lengths on me. I remember thinking at one time: "Christ, I'm never going to catch him now." But Grundy fought back like a lion. When we started to motor I was sure that Grundy would do it. When we went up to Bustino I thought: "I've got you." Then he fought back and I had to pull out all I had got. Grundy was exhausted but he gave me everything that day, his whole body worked for me. I shall remember him as the horse who simply threw himself at the line to win that day. When we went past the post I eased Grundy immediately. I sensed that he was completely whacked. Really, you know, but for losing those four lengths on the final turn I would have won much easier. When Bustino headed off for home like that I did not think we would win. Then I did not know who would get it, until Grundy battled on the second time. I reckon Bustino died about 100 yards from the stick and that's what decided it.' After the race Mercer said: 'Don't forget that we are giving Grundy a stone today. There cannot be a horse alive who could give Grundy a stone and hope to live with him. The pace was red hot and my horse just faltered in the last 100 yards. It was fantastic. He was so brave. He broke the track record giving away a stone. He ran a hell of a race. We gave the people something they'll never forget. It can't be bad, can it?'

Carlo Vittadini immediately estimated that Grundy's value had gone to nearly three million pounds. He said: 'Of course I do not regret selling him for a million pounds. I am pleased for England and your bloodstock breeders. It is true that Grundy has such an unusual colour that I did not really like him much. But I was keen on his conformation and breeding. If he had not been such a strange colour he would have gone for much more than 11 000 guineas and I don't suppose I would ever have bought him. He looks more like a horse for a cowboy than a jockey.' It was certainly a great day for the Vittadini family. His daughter Franca won the opening race on the card, the Sierra Leone Diamond Stakes on Hard April, which was also trained by Peter Walwyn. Franca worked at Henry Cecil's stable for a period.

Like her father she has striking blue eyes, fair hair and a strong nose. Eddery completed a memorable day for Peter Walwyn's all-conquering team when he steered home Inchmarlo, a comfortable winner of the Virginia Water Stakes in the race bang after the King George VI.

Vittadini stated that he was keen to allow his chestnut colt to bow out in the Champion Stakes at Newmarket. But the arrangement with the National Stud was that he could have two more possible races at this stage. So the attraction of running Grundy in the Benson and Hedges at York just twenty-four days later was an obvious one. Of Grundy's Ascot win John Sharratt, by now becoming a big fan, noted in *Raceform*: 'Grundy was superb. Always very relaxed, despite the blistering pace, he was two or three lengths down on Bustino coming round the home turn and then, when asked for an effort, showed his true qualities. He fought his way to the front with a furlong to run and needed all his courage and resolution to battle off the runner-up. There can be no doubt that he is a true champion.' I suppose you would have been led away by gentlemen in white coats if you had looked down on Grundy and Bustino after the race and said that neither of them would ever win another race in their lives. Bustino was retired to stud, anyway, although the plan after the race was to send him over to Longchamp for the Arc de Triomphe. 'I think Grundy broke his heart,' was Joe Mercer's final verdict. Bustino sustained an injury and the memory of him having to give in to Grundy on the line is the last we are left with.

History was against sending Grundy to York for the Benson and Hedges Gold Cup. This race was first run in 1972 and every year, bar one, had produced a turn-up. But most important of all was the lesson of Brigadier Gerard. In 1972 he had a far, far easier task than Grundy in winning the King George. He was 'let loose' by Joe Mercer well over a furlong out and had no trouble in accounting for Parnell by 1½ lengths. Yet he was sent north only to be well trounced, without a single excuse, by Roberto, although I would admit that it was a peculiar race. So the dashing Brigadier had tried the King George–Benson and Hedges double and had his colours lowered for the first time in his career. Was Grundy really going to attempt to win where the Brigadier had been beaten so sensationally by three lengths? At the end of the season Peter Walwyn, with whom the decision largely rested, was man enough to admit: 'It was a mistake to ever run Grundy at York.' I think that Keith Freeman was against the idea but Grundy had done well at home after the race. Looking back Freeman said: 'After the Ascot race I asked a doctor whether an athlete who attains fabulous perfection on the racetrack is ever able to do so again within a short time. I was thinking of Roger Bannister's four-minute mile. The doctor said that he thought horses were like athletes and it was possible to overstretch themselves. Roger Bannister was never able to reproduce that kind of running and Grundy, who had a rating of 144 with *Timeform* after Ascot, was rather like that. He had gone at Ascot as far as was equinely possible.' Both Grundy and Bustino stretched well beyond their zenith but nobody realized that Grundy had probably been done irreparable damage.

Peter Diamond recalls: 'Shortly after that Ascot race Pat Eddery came down to the Overbury Stud as he was very keen to see Grundy's mare. I asked him how Grundy had recovered from the race and he said that he thought that he was in better condition then than he had ever been at any stage of his career.' Indeed Eddery said: 'We were certain that he was okay. I rode him at work and he felt just as good, if not better. He looked great and I was keen to have a go in the Benson and Hedges.' It is racing history now that, while Grundy was second twice in his career and won all his eight other races, at York he was only able to finish a sad fourth. Writing on August 19th the day of the race, in the *Sporting Life* George Ennor started his preview by saying: 'It would be ridiculous to put anything to beat Grundy in the Benson and Hedges Gold Cup at York today.' But ridiculous or not the sensation happened and Grundy joined Rheingold and Brigadier Gerard as three top-class performers on whom the gods did not shine brightly at the Knavesmire. At Ascot Grundy beat Dahlia by $5\frac{1}{2}$ lengths. Card King was $7\frac{1}{2}$ lengths back in fifth and Star Appeal was $22\frac{1}{2}$ lengths adrift.

But like the so-called 'good things' before him, Grundy bit the dust and the formbook was made to look irrelevant. Dahlia, given a masterful ride by Lester Piggott, won by 1½ lengths from Card King, with Star Appeal five lengths away third and Grundy a further four lengths away fourth.

Seeing the video of the Benson and Hedges is, for me at least, like watching a fluke last-minute goal knocking your favourite side out of the FA Cup or seeing your favourite boxer trying in vain to beat the dreaded count. For those of us who came to love Grundy it does not make happy viewing. Four furlongs out Lester Piggott's famous backside can be seen as Dahlia led the field. Was he riding a waiting race, or simply trying to make the best of it on the once great Dahlia? We were soon to find out. Three furlongs out Pat Eddery moved Grundy in a position to challenge. Two furlongs out the writing was painted in large letters on the wall and ITV commentator John Penney observed: 'Grundy looks to be in trouble as they pass the two-furlong marker.' Eddery picked up his whip and waved it down Grundy's side but never actually hit him. The champion jockey gave Grundy a tender farewell, which was certainly deserved. As Grundy faded out of the firing-line and Piggott stormed off for home with a renewed burst it was the ex-selling plater Card King who flashed past the famous Vittadini colours to finish second. Only French raider Meautry and the moderate handicapper Jimsun finished behind Grundy. And that was a near thing, but for a neck and half a length Grundy, who went in the betting from 3–1 on to 9–4 on, would have finished last. I can think of few more harrowing sights than that of a true champion getting beaten when circumstances rather than his opponents have contributed to his downfall. But it must have been a real hammer blow for Walwyn and Eddery. Recalled Pat: 'He looked good on the course and felt okay until we got to the last three furlongs and the pressure was on. That's when the heat was on us and in two or three strides I could tell the old spark had gone. I was determined not to bash him about if he could not win. It was a sad farewell.' Grundy came back into the winners' enclosure to a hushed reception. The rapturous Ascot greeting had changed to a stunned silence. However, the achievement of Dahlia must not be overlooked. Piggott rode a peach of a race, waiting in front and then going on again. But it was clear Grundy's Ascot battle contributed to his York downfall. If he had been able to talk I am sure he would have requested a rest. But his courage was such that he probably continued to star on the gallops and gave no real hint that his strength was sapped. He kidded those nearest to him that he was still at peak fitness. At Ascot Grundy beat Dahlia by a little more than five lengths. At York he was ten lengths behind her in fourth place. The turn-round of fifteen lengths showed that the Grundy who trailed in at York was a mere shadow of his superb self.

'That's racing. This sort of thing has happened before,' was Walwyn's philosophic reaction. 'Of course he had a very hard race in the King George but he came back so well afterwards that I was sure it was all right to run him today. I wouldn't have done so otherwise. I had no doubts before the race and it is only now he's beaten that I very much regret it. It was clear two furlongs out that he was not going to beat Dahlia and it was pointless Pat giving Grundy a hard race.' Carlo Vittadini said: 'Walwyn is the top trainer in the country. He obviously thought that Grundy was well. It's too early to say whether Grundy will ever run again. Personally I would like to see him end his career on a winning note in the Champion Stakes.' Lester Piggott said: 'Dahlia was better than last year when she won the race. I knew that I would win from two furlongs out.' Neither Nelson Bunker Hunt nor Maurice Zilber were present, a clear indication that they did not really think that Dahlia would repeat her success. Anne's Pretender did not run because of a passport irregularity and Ryan Price incurred a £275 fine for not presenting the passport at the course. Price was ordered to pay half a percent of the stake money under a new rule. The venture cost more than this as, having realized that the passport was still at Findon, a plane was chartered to try and get it to the course in time. But they just failed and Anne's Pretender was not allowed to run. Passports were not a subject to mention to the Findon maestro at this time as he was somewhat waspish about the whole affair.

Grundy's running at York has sparked off many after-race discussions. As Walwyn admits it was a mistake to run him there, but his handler would never have contemplated the move if Grundy had not looked so well at home. But the fact remains – sadly for all time in the record books – that just three and a half weeks after giving his all at Ascot he ran some fifteen lengths below his best in the Benson and Hedges. Now the question arose as to whether Grundy should ever see another racecourse in his life. Having won £312 122 for Carlo Vittadini – remember he cost just 11 000 guineas – he had clearly become a huge money-spinner for all concerned. And the budget had been further boosted when the National Stud, through the Levy Board, paid £750 000 to buy a three-quarter share in him two weeks before the Irish Derby. The attraction, therefore, of seeking the £36 000 first prize in the Champion Stakes at Newmarket on October 18th seemed remote. But Vittadini had said that he was keen to see his wonderful champion end his career on a winning note and his feelings were understandable. He did not want Grundy to go to stud with his final outing being the only real scar on his whole career, the sad fourth at York. Grundy had become a national hero. His York defeat could be put down solely to the Ascot contest. But another below-par performance would have done obvious damage to his potential stud reputation.

Newmarket's Champion Stakes is another fascinating race where some truly great horses have been beaten. The race, first run in 1877, has proved a graveyard to 'hot-pots' in recent years – rather similar to the Benson and Hedges Gold Cup. Brigadier Gerard won in 1971 and made a winning farewell to his fabulous career a year later, when starting at 3–1 on. But Nijinsky was beaten into second place by Charles St George's Lorenzaccio in 1970 and in 1973 Allez France, at the very peak of her career, finished second to the mode-rate Irish-trained Hurry Harriet. The prospect of seeing Grundy trailing in behind a lesser animal was not a pleasing one. And after a dry summer it was clear that a wet autumn was on the way and the going could easily have been soft at Newmarket, which was another factor which would have counted against Grundy. All in all, he had nothing to gain by running at Newmarket . . . and everything to lose.

Nearly two years to the day when he was led round the Newmarket sales ring the big decision was made. It was on October 5th, 1973, that the yearling with the colour nobody liked had gone under the hammer. On September 30th, 1975, after long telephone discussions between Vittadini, Walwyn and Freeman in Italy and England it was decided that Grundy had run his last race. Pat Eddery rode the great horse in a deciding gallop and reported that the old sparkle had really gone. I was fortunate enough to hear of the likely outcome of the vital talks. The *Sun* carried a streamer headline saying: 'Goodbye Grundy.' Below this was a sub-heading which I think revealed all our feelings: 'Let him bow out as a champ.' The next day the Press Association issued one of their 'rush' releases to all newspapers. At 13.50 hours the PA Racing Rush said simply: 'Grundy will not race again.' This was one of the first days at the PA under the control of the new Racing Editor, David Staveley, who was formerly on the PA service in the Law Courts. The fact that Grundy's retirement warranted a 'rush' release is interesting. The most urgent PA news is sent out as a 'flash'. Next important is the 'rush' and then a 'snap'.

Grundy had looked perfect in the paddock at York but his stable lad, and number one admirer, Charlie Johnson, had sensed that something was wrong with the colt for the first time in their highly successful union. He recalls: 'Usually when Grundy had been transported to the races he was inclined to get quite excited by the time we got to the other end of the journey. We had to park the lorry so that when he came down the ramp he could not buck and kick into anything. That morning I can remember us doing the same routine. We were all waiting for the fireworks but when the ramp was lowered he came out as quiet as an old sheep. He came down the ramp and did not give a single kick. Usually he gave a right performance.'

It was the day after the Epsom Derby when plans were

first made to see that Grundy continued to stay in England and was not lost to foreign shores. Keith Freeman said: 'I telephoned Sir Desmond Plummer, head of the Levy Board, the morning after the Epsom Derby. He realized the importance of keeping Grundy in England and I stressed that we did not want to lose him abroad. We wanted to see lots more little Grundys running about the place in England. When the National Stud bought Habat I am sure they already had one eye on Grundy as he was unbeaten at that time at the end of his two-year-old career.' It was Lt-Col Douglas Gray, who, before he retired as director of the National Stud, was especially keen to get Grundy. He joked: 'I must admit that obtaining Habat was something of a sprat to catch a mackerel.'

Recent trends in international breeding have tended to show a marked leaning towards the blue-bloods produced by the North American breeders. At the Keeneland sales the yearlings which are often the most sought after are the ones which were household names in Britain. But the swing of the financial pendulum has meant that so many of our great horses have been whisked away across the Atlantic. The success of Sir Ivor, Nijinsky and Vaguely Noble will never be forgotten. But it is highly unlikely that this terrific trio will ever tread on British soil again. Now they are all in Kentucky and it will obviously be several years before English-bred colts can match these kind of parents. The majority of the best horses in British racing in the late sixties and early seventies were bought by foreign breeders. Now the situation has changed a little and it is wonderful to think that Brigadier Gerard, Mill Reef and Grundy are making love at Newmarket and not in the blue-grass fields of Kentucky. At the National Stud Grundy was the fourth Derby winner. The others were Never Say Die, Blakeney and Mill Reef. Sadly on November 28th, 1975, Never Say Die had to be put down and there are now three Derby heroes at the Stud. On July 23rd, 1975 nineteen of the shares in Grundy were balloted. Among the British breeders who have a share in Grundy are Lord Howard de Walden and Major Michael Wyatt, Lord Porchester, Lord Rotherwick, Sir Philip Oppenheimer (whose firm De Beers sponsored the King George VI), Jim Joel, Colonel Roger and Mrs Hue-Williams and Lavinia, Duchess of Norfolk.

On Tuesday, October 21st, 1975 Grundy left Seven Barrows bound for his new career at the National Stud, which is positioned close to the July Course at Newmarket. It was a sentimental moment for Walwyn, Eddery, Mc-Cormack and his lad Johnson. As his beloved star was 'boxed up' for the last time in his life Walwyn said: 'He has been a great servant. We shall miss him one hell of a lot and I have warned the National Stud that I will be pestering them to see him whenever I can at Newmarket.' For Eddery – the first of his Derby winners – it was an especially sentimental moment. He entered Grundy's box and kissed his hero. To say that there was not a hint of a tear would be incorrect. 'To think I will never see him in the stable again,' reflected Pat at the time. Later he told me: 'It was horrible to see him go. I couldn't really believe that as he was led away he would never have a saddle on his back ever again. Horses like that come only once in a lifetime and that's the sad part about it.

'But I was lucky to be the only man who ever rode him in public. As I say, the Derby will always be my race with him. But in the King George he gave me everything. He threw himself at the line and that's why I shall always love him.'

12. 'This is my love'

'Is this the end of life as we know it?' The speaker, one of the revered members of the racing Establishment press, was perfectly serious as he gazed almost unbelievingly out across Newmarket Heath. The day was May 1st, 1975. The occasion was the 1,000 Guineas and the spectacle which had caused my colleague to stare in amazement was a human wall of striking stable lads completely blocking the course.

Newmarket had never seen anything like this. The Battle of Newmarket was under way. When the jockeys decided to break their ranks on their way to the start for the 2.30 race it was quickly called the Charge of the Light Brigade. When the die-hards watching could stand no more and decided to get involved in a pitched battle with the strikers, it was dubbed the Charge of the Old Brigade. But what happened at headquarters that day was the result of a straight clash between the local trainers and stable lads, over their conditions and wages.

Their decision to stage a demonstration was just an all too familiar phase of modern-day life. But there had never been anything like this before and the ugly scars which were left from the memory of Newmarket at the Guineas meeting can only be matched by the Suffragette incident during the 1913 Epsom Derby when Emily Davison hurled herself under King George V's horse at Tattenham Corner and was killed.

Jockeys were unable to get to the start for the 2.30 race as the lads had staged a sit-in completely across the course. Recalls Bruce Raymond: 'We were circling around and could not get through. Then Lester Piggott said: "Let's charge," so I went through with Lester and Greville Starkey. They were trying to hang on to our legs but we charged on through.' But Willie Carson was not so lucky and was dragged from Pericet. He said: 'They grabbed me and pulled me off my horse. They snatched the whip from my hands and I was hit across the back and left thigh. I was a stable lad myself seventeen years ago, earning half a crown a week, but after that I lost all sympathy with the strikers.'

Carson waved at people in the stands to come to his aid and this was when the Establishment cleared the rails and set off towards the drama area. Among this counter rally was General Sir Randle Feilden, aged seventy-four, the former Senior Steward of the Jockey Club.

The stable lads' strike was eventually ended on July 24th. Much bitterness had been created by the actions of both parties. In the end it was agreed that the lads should receive thirty-seven pounds a week. Said John Winter, the spokesman for the trainers: 'Thank God it is all over. The ten lads I have sacked will not be able to come back because my yard has been cut from sixty-seven to forty horses and there is no place for them.' Whatever the rights or wrongs of the dispute – and I was always rather sympathetic with the lads in their cause – Sam Horncastle did emerge as a national figure during the union bargaining.

There was not much humour when the strike was on. A possee of lads visited Ascot one day and were allowed to organize a march up the straight. 'Winter out. Winter out' was their cry and it must be said that it was unfortunate for likable John Winter that he had to be the figurehead of the Trainers' Federation for the first year when all this trouble broke out. Bitterness crept in when Henry Cecil said that Tom Dickie, the lad who looked after Bolkonski before going on strike, would not receive his cut from the 2,000 Guineas win. On the day of the famous sit-in one press colleague told me solemnly: 'It is a terrible thing when horses are stopped at Newmarket.' I could not resist replying: 'Don't be so shocked. They have been stopping horses at Newmarket for centuries.'

Often there is not enough humour in racing. There was a little example of good-hearted fun when No Alimony won the Craven Stakes at Newmarket in 1975. It reminded journalist Richard Baerlein of an article had had written the previous autumn. After one race he wrote that he 'would go to work if No Alimony could not beat Grundy at any distance from a mile upwards'. He was soon to receive a telegram saying: 'Go to work.' It was signed: 'Grundy, Seven Barrows, Lambourn.' There was even a touch of humour from Lester Piggott on the eve of his great title battle with Eddery in 1974. The two contestants for the title were gathered in a Manchester hotel for film interviews. Uncertain of which way the title was going to go, television whizz-kids were keen to be covered both ways. They wanted to arrange two talk-ins, one with Lester as the champion and the other with Pat as the winner. Lester wouldn't fall for it. The camera kept rolling but each time the unsmiling maestro said: 'That's not right. I am going to be the champion.' Yards of film was wasted but Piggott would not assume the role of the runner-up, which he subsequently had to do at Haydock the next day.

There was another funny moment at Newmarket towards the end of the 1975 season. A trainer and his wife were invited by the Jockey Club into their private rooms after winning one of the big sponsored races. 'Well done,' said a Jockey Club enthusiast to the wife, 'I do hope your husband had a good bet.' 'No,' came the reply, 'he hasn't had a bet since he retired as a jockey.'

By the end of the 1975 season it was clear that there still remained a curious paradox in racing. Owners and trainers had said all year tht they simply could not afford to pay the lads any more money. 'There just isn't the money in the game any longer' was the excuse. Yet, in the sales rings of Goffs and Newmarket, records were being broken as though money was going out of business. Vincent O'Brien shattered the European yearling price when he paid 127000 guineas for a colt by champions Northern Dancer and What a Threat. Then at Newmarket Robin Hastings of the British Blood-stock Agency went to a shattering 202000 guineas for a son of Mill Reef. As usual there was the after-bidding secrecy as to the identity of the new owner. But anybody who had seen Lady Beaverbrook after the sale could not fail to guess who was behind the buying. Jack Doyle, who usually buys close to 300 yearlings each autumn, did not rate this Mill Reef colt. 'I would not have him on my mind,' said Jack, probably the best judge of horseflesh in the game.

So, the 1975 season was an odd one. Stable lads having to strike before they could get a wage increase. Sir Desmond Plummer having to hold a heavily loaded political pistol at racing before they would get their house in order. Ravi Tikkoo deciding to take his horses to France and certain trainers having to cut their strings by a half.

But for Pat Eddery this was the year of Grundy and his second championship win. Before he ever changed into the silks in England Pat was 2–1 on to regain his title. He won the second race of the Flat season on Solid Silver and never looked back. He was never headed and at the start of the season struck a good partnership with Malton trainer Frank Carr. After riding Solid Silver for Carr, Pat completed a first-day double when he won the final race on Just Revenge for Atty Corbett. Wins on Understudy and Hilarious the next day – Walwyn's first two runners of the season – maintained his good average. Gloss, attempting to lump a record-breaking top weight of 9 st 8 lb to victory in the Lincoln, finished well down the field with Eddery, but yet again Doncaster proved a lucky kick-off. When Pat had his first ever winner at Teesside, Doubtful Number for Frank Carr, he further increased his lead and at that stage Carr had saddled six winners from only eleven runners. At no time did Eddery look remotely like being caught and at the end of the season his score was a personal best of 164. Willie Carson was next with 131, although he had thirty-two more rides. Pat chalked up his hundredth winner of the season on the filly Acquire at Warwick on August 7th. This ended a frustrating run on ninety-nine for him, but it was still his fastest century. His first 100 came in September, 1973 on Fragrant Air for Dermot Whelan. In 1974 he reached the 100 on Mick Masson's Reine Beau at Goodwood on August 24th. So

Eddery reached the 'ton' for the first time on a Peter Walwyn horse, when his superb skills got Acquire home by a length on firm going which she did not really like.

Grundy's glorious campaign stole the limelight but Pat still had many more big race successes. Silky, the daughter of Nijinsky who had made a simply fabulous debut at Newmarket, never quite realized her potential and Pat was well beaten on her in the 1,000 Guineas. Before the race she was reported to be 'pulling up trees on the gallops' but I suspect that she was in fact a difficult filly to train.

After the success of Polygamy the previous year, Louis Freedman was hoping that his One Over Parr would prove a top-class filly. She was an encouraging third behind Rose Bowl in the Nell Gwyn Stakes and then won the Cheshire Oaks, beating Shallow Stream and Brilliantine. In the Oaks she was second favourite at 11–2 but could only finish sixth and was actually beaten by her stable companion May Hill, who finished fourth with Frank Morby riding. A win in the Lancashire Oaks at Haydock raised hopes that she might win the Irish Guinness Oaks. There was a triple blinkered raid by English fillies to the Curragh. Juliette Marny, who wore blinkers for the first time when she and Lester won the Epsom Oaks, again wore them. They were also used for the first time on One Over Parr and Val's Girl. But again Piggott picked the right one and, discarding Nobiliary, went for the neck winner Juliette Marny. One Over Parr was twelfth and did not race again.

May Hill was another good filly for Walwyn and Eddery. She wanted soft going and certainly did not get it in the Epsom Oaks when she finished fourth. Owner Percival Williams said: 'She did not like the firm going at Epsom and all around the top corner was hating it. But when she got on the ground that had been watered she simply flew and was finishing very well.' May Hill subsequently won a two-horse race at Haydock before beating the 2–1 on Juliette Marny in the Yorkshire Oaks. Then in the Park Hill Stakes at Doncaster she was faced by the highly-rated Vincent O'Brien raider, Tuscarora. Commentating on the race for ITV was Raleigh Gilbert, who said in the closing stages:

'Lester Piggott has to get out his whip to ride Tuscarora. But Pat Eddery has not moved a muscle on May Hill. Tuscarora can't live with May Hill and the long-striding Tipperary filly is beaten. This is Peter Walwyn's hundredth winner of the season.' At the line May Hill won by a comfortable $1\frac{1}{2}$ lengths.

Although Walwyn had enjoyed great success with his senior horses, by the beginning of the autumn he was worried that he might not have a really top-class two-year-old. But his fears were well trounced when Pasty made it five wins on the trot to take the William Hill Cheveley Park Stakes at Newmarket. Pasty, also owned by Percival Williams, was sprinter-sired by Raffingora but her dam Ma Marie should produce the stamina required. Wins with Pasty and May Hill brought Williams's winnings to £70000. Just after the Cheveley, Peter Walwyn, more than usually delighted by his success, quipped: 'English racing is not all that bad if you've got good horses.' Pasty was duly made winter ante-post favourite for the 1,000 Guineas. Her win, aided by the usual Eddery coolness, brought Walwyn's winnings to past the £500000 mark for the season. Pasty was still inexperienced, despite her four previous wins, and missed the break and lost four lengths. But she soon made up the deficit on the wide outside and won by two necks from Dame Foolish and Solar. Williams has his own ideas about breeding and Walwyn was a little alarmed to find Pasty running around as a yearling in a field bordered by barbed wire. Walwyn suggested to Williams that it might be more sensible to keep his young horse in a railed paddock but was given the straight reply: 'There's an awful lot of barbed wire around Lambourn so the yearlings might just as well get used to it here in case they get loose in training.'

Patch's ten lengths' win in the Lingfield Derby Trial stamped him as a top-class performer. But he was just pipped by Val de l'Orne in the French Derby at Chantilly by a head. But for this narrow defeat Patch would have completed a fabulous fourth Derby win for Carlo Vittadini in the same year as Grundy (English and Irish) and Orange Bay (Italian) carried the famous blue and yellow colours to victory. Patch was subsequently beaten in the Grand Prix de Paris at Longchamp. The fickle Paris crowd were quick to cat-call Eddery, who was forced to go to the front very early on. Patch led into the straight but was overtaken by the winner Matahawk and subsequently finished seventh. Always a hard-puller he tugged his way to the front too early to run an ideal race and Walwyn said: 'Pat couldn't help it. This horse has always been a hard-puller ever since he joined me from Italy during the winter. He has run away with other jockeys before now.' Patch again made all when he pipped Sea Anchor by half a length in the Great Voltiguer Stakes at York. He was widely regarded as Pat's automatic ride for the St Leger but he skipped that event and his final race of the season was the Cumberland Lodge Stakes at Ascot when he finished a disappointing fifth behind Calaba. He was considered as a possible Arc de Triomphe runner and had also been invited to run in the Washington International at Laurel Park. But after the Ascot defeat Walwyn said: 'I think it is very unlikely that he will run again this season. He takes too much out of himself during a race and must learn to settle. But he does stay in training for next year.'

When experts assumed that Eddery would pick Patch for the St Leger, the young Irishman had already ridden Consol in a trial gallop and been greatly impressed. Because Pat thought Consol was the better prospect Walwyn decided to take out Patch and run the former. Said Peter: 'P. Eddery tells me that Consol is the one and that's good enough for me. It is very seldom that P. Eddery makes the wrong choice. He has ridden them both recently and this is the one he wants to ride at Doncaster.' There was to be no fairy-tale ending here as Consol finished fifth behind the runaway Bruni, who thrashed King Pellinore by 10 lengths. Eddery was the early leader on Consol but was soon under pressure. As the field turned into the straight some racegoers were seen scampering right scross the course, an event which prompted a concerned Raleigh Gilbert on ITV to exclaim: 'What in the world is going on?' Later, as Bruni coasted home, he said: 'It's Bruni running away with it now. Lester Piggott has chosen the wrong one.' Piggott was second on King Pellinore.

At Haydock Park on November 12th, 1975, the Flat season ended. The previous year the championship could still have been won by Eddery or Piggott on the very last day. This time the title was all 'done and dusted'. With 164 winners, Eddery was way ahead of Carson (131) and Piggott (113). The previous year Lester's percentage had been noticeably better. But Pat showed that he had closed the gap in this respect. His percentage of winning rides was a magnificent 20.07, while Lester was only fractionally better with 21.52. The year proved a clean sweep for Eddery's connections. Carlo Vittadini was far and away the leading owner, his six horses having won £209 492. Another Italian, Carlo d'Alessio – from the Henry Cecil camp – was second, his three horses winning £125 558. The Overbury Stud, which produced Grundy, topped the breeders' list with seven horses winning £194 480. And to complete the fabulous year Peter Walwyn's sixty-nine winning horses scored 121 successes in England, worth £382 527 – a really brilliant achievement. Great Nephew, sire of Grundy, proved the leading sire and sixteen of his offspring won twenty-nine races worth £291 048. It was success, success all the way.

What now of the future? What are the ambitions of a man who has achieved so much so soon? Pat told me: 'I just want to keep on riding well. I have no weight problems at present, although I still have to be a little careful. I never eat bread or potatoes. I have plenty of fish and meat. Never vegetables, I don't like them much. I have installed a sauna bath at my home but this is more to keep me fit than to keep my weight down. I usually have twenty minutes in the sauna every day when I am at home. It's bloody boring sometimes so I usually take my shaving gear in with me and have a shave.

'I admit that I have been very lucky and so much has happened in a short time. I do often think that everything could go wrong and it is frightening to think that I could tumble back down the ladder. It's always in your mind that it could happen. But I aim to just keep going and ride more and more winners. Peter Walwyn has been very loyal to me. I know that the papers say that I earn as much as £30 000 a year. You have only to look at the value of the races which I have won to see that I am obviously making a lot of money. But the tax man takes a lot too. I just hope to keep going as I am. Being champion is a terrific thrill. Only one problem is people who pester me for tips. All our horses always do their best.'

Of his rival jockeys Eddery is complimentary. 'Lester's unique,' he admits. 'Some of the other jockeys talk to him about their horses. Lester loves to know what they all think. I never speak to him about horses. It is pointless trying to copy his style because nobody will ever be able to ride like him. I also rate Willie Carson and Geoff Lewis very highly, while I think Greville Starkey is very underrated and his win in the Arc de Triomphe on Star Appeal proved this.'

Which of all Pat's wins has given him the greatest satisfaction? Which was his best ever display in the saddle? Says Eddery: 'I think of all the races I have won the one which thrilled me most, strictly from the race riding point of view, was when I won the Britannia Stakes at Royal Ascot on Tudor Rhythm in 1973. He had won his three previous races but I really had to give him a hard race to win that day. I can remember it so well as it made me top jockey at the Royal meeting. Two furlongs out I seemed to have no chance but I got to work on him and won by a head, bang on the line. That was my best win.' Father Jimmy Eddery thinks that another win at Ascot was Pat's best ever display. 'Winning on English Prince in the King Edward VII was the one I shall always remember,' says Jimmy; 'they went a blistering pace that day but Pat was never ruffled.' Peter Walwyn, the man who has masterminded so many of the thrilling last gasp wins, is hard pushed to select one especially memorable ride. 'There are so many,' he says, 'but I suppose the best one for me was when he won on Cesarea by a head at Sandown in September 1973. He just won it in the final strides.' Ironically Cesarea was the last horse Duncan Keith ever rode for Walwyn.

For my money the best ever display I saw from Eddery was on State Occasion, when he won the Horris Hill Stakes at Newbury in 1975 by ¾ length from Seadiver. From two furlongs out Eddery came with a perfectly timed run and State Occasion got his head in front just close to home. It was sheer perfection. At the end of 1975 State Occasion and Oats were rated by Pat as the best two-year-old colts he had ridden, while Pasty was obviously the pick of the ladies. Ironically the Horris Hill Stakes of 1972 had seen a far from perfect ride from Eddery. He left Midsummer Star a great deal to do and was a fast finishing second behind Long Row, although he was travelling much better in the dying stages. Mick Masson trained Midsummer Star. He was told by owner Bernard Walsh to go to 12500 guineas for him but took a chance and got him for 13500 guineas. When Eddery won the Tankvervile Nursery on him at Ascot he not only beat the highly-rated son of Sir Ivor, Cavo Doro, he also smashed the existing two-year-old record over seven furlongs. But in the Horris Hill he had to be satisfied with second. Later in his reliable career he was second in the Irish 2,000 Guineas. In the autumn of 1975 Keith Freeman arranged for him to go to stud in South Africa. Said Mick's wife Sally: 'All our horses are mint mad. I have to go to the cash-and-carry place once a month to buy ten big cases of mints. Midsummer Star was especially keen and when he went to South Africa we sent a case of mints with him.' The Barn Stables at Lewes were previously the home of that great horsemaster Tom Masson. Now son Mick is keeping up the family tradition and amongst the inmates at Barn Stables is a parrot called 'Cocky', who has the odd habit of screeching 'Bloody Owners' every time the telephone rings. He must have learnt this years ago as Mick now has a delightful set of owners.

Having asked Pat which was his best ever riding display it was only fair to pose the question the other way round – which was the worst? He answered quickly: 'Charlie Bubbles in the Dee Stakes at Chester in 1974. Chester is a tricky course and you have always got to be well up with the leaders. That day I gave Charlie Bubbles far too much to do and we got no nearer than fifth behind Averof. I was very sorry but I did not get a bollicking from the guv'nor. He accepted that I had ridden a bad race.' Charlie Bubbles went on to give Pat the five-hundredth winner of his career when he won the Newbury Spring Cup on April 19th 1975.

Raceform expert and BBC TV paddock commentator, John Hanmer, has few equals when it comes to racereading and has a unique ability for spotting the smallest details in races. He says: 'I think Eddery rides with more consistency at his age than Piggott did. He was inclined to be brilliant but a little erratic. The great thing about Eddery is that he is completely ambidexterous. He can pick up his whip with either hand, which many top jockeys are unable to do. Piggott is far better with his right hand but can use both. Willie Carson, Sandy Barclay, Jeff King and Terry Biddlecombe are all in the right-hand only class. David Mould was the odd one out. He was far better using his left hand. Tony Murray, Joe Mercer and Geoff Lewis are like Eddery – ambidexterous. Joe Mercer is the best at using the stick in either hand. He has never rung up for a ride in his life and I think he is better than Piggott or Eddery but nobody will probably agree with me. To me his win on Counsel at York in 1957 was the greatest display of riding I ever saw. Joe on Bustino in the Coronation Cup was poetry in motion. Also on Highclere when beating Eddery on Polygamy in the 1,000 Guineas and in defeat on Homeric by Mill Reef in the Coronation Cup.' And the worst he has ever witnessed? 'David Yates once being beaten on a red hot favourite trained by Fulke Johnson Houghton at Brighton. It was a work of art to get beaten on that one, although he was trying for his life. He went clear and never spotted somebody coming up on his inner.

'Age is no barrier in jockeyship but I think Mercer has pulled more races out of the fire than any other jockey. Eddery is like Gordon Richards used to be. He likes to have his horses always in the first four or five and then move up to challenge two furlongs out.'

I have heard it said that Jimmy Eddery was a hard rider, a man not averse to using his whip unsparingly in a hectic finish. This cannot be said of Pat, who if a horse is good enough will always give him a beautifully balanced 'hands and heels' ride. Says Pat: 'In my career I have only had five whips of my own. I never like using a long whip. They hurt horses and I prefer the smaller, lighter ones. If you give a horse a caning with the big coshes they may win one day but they never come back the same. They have memories and just curl up. I prefer to give them a flick with my short whip.'

Pat, who has ridden winners in England, Ireland, France, Germany, Sweden, Norway, Hong Kong, South Africa and Kenya, has always regarded Ascot as his favourite course. He is hard pushed to explain exactly why but says: 'I just think it's a lovely, super place.' His home is just half a mile away from his best adviser Frenchie Nicholson on the outskirts of Cheltenham. 'He still gives me advice and I always listen to everything he tells me,' says Pat. His nearest hotel is the Hotel de la Bere at Southam, Cheltenham, a wonderful old manor house which has been converted. Says the manager, fellow Irishman Kevin O'Rourke: 'Pat walks round from his home practically every night and buys four or five Romeo and Juliet cigars. He really loves them. If he can't come down himself he sends one of his family out for them. I once said to him that he was silly to keep coming round for four or five cigars a night. I said that I could get him a box of fifty. He said: "That would be ostentatious." That's the kind of chap he is. Very modest. He often sits in the corner of the hotel bar and has one drink. Unless you knew him you would never suspect that he was the champion jockey.' It is at the Hotel de la Bere that Eddery has organized private celebration parties after his two years as champion jockey. Dashing straight from the final day of the Flat at Haydock Park, he throws a party on the Wednesday night for his close personal friends.

While not having the same weight problems as Lester, Pat, a whip-cord of 5 ft 1 in, has to be careful. 'I can keep down to 8 st 1 lb and 8 st 2 lb without too much trouble,' he says. 'I don't have to kill myself to make these weights.' Says Frenchie Nicholson: 'We like our boys to ride with a pound or two in hand. We would never allow them to risk their health by wasting. On Mondays we only accept rides for Pat around 8 st 2 lb, and would only accept anything around 7 st 13 lb later in the week. Then it would only be around the last two races on the card when he had already lost a pound or two through his efforts in earlier races.'

At the end of the 1975 campaign Pat had only a few days rest before he dashed off to South Africa, on to Singapore, and then back to South Africa. I asked him if he had ever thought about what he will do when he finally retires, many years ahead we all sincerely hope. Had he thought about training? He said: 'I haven't really thought much about training. It's a long way ahead. I just want to improve my riding. You know, I enjoy riding out for the guv'nor as much as I do winning races. It's great to get there early in the morning and sit on different horses every time. You may have some moderate old thing, or suddenly ride one two-year-old and think: "This is one hell of a nice horse." Sometimes you ride one you have never seen before and love the feel of him straight away. It's a great atmosphere. We have a good breakfast afterwards. Someone is always cracking jokes. I enjoy this part of the set-up. Far away from the racecourses, when there is not a punter in sight, I finally discover my true love of racing – simply galloping horses across the downs. There's always the chance that I will get the leg up for the first time on another Grundy.'

And who better to ride him than Patrick Eddery?

Index

Compiled by M. Prior

187

191